TOEIC

Extended

TOEIC Extended

1 TOEIC이란?

TOEIC은 Test of English for International Communication의 약어로 국제적 의사소통 능력을 측정하기 위한 영어 시험이다. TOEIC의 문제 작성 및 채점은, 미국의 New Jersey에 본부를 둔 ETS(Educational Testing Service)가 시행하고 있다. TOEIC의 최초 테스트는 1979년 12월에 일본에서 실시되었다. TOEFL(Test of English as a Foreign Language)이 미국의 대학에 진학하기 위한 영어 능력 테스트라면 TOEIC은 기업체의 사원이나 일반인들의 영어 능력을 평가하기 위해서 이용되고 있다. 따라서 생활 영어나 비즈니스 영어가 주축을 이루고 있다. TOEIC의 큰 특징은 TOFEL과 마찬가지로 합격, 불합격을 결정하는 것이 아니라 시험 결과가 점수로 표시된다. 우리 나라에서는 1982년 1월에 처음 시행되었고, 요즈음은 대기업 및 중소기업의 신입사원 선발과 승진 심사는 물론 각종 국가고시에도 영어시험을 TOEIC 성적으로 대체하고 있다.

2 TOEIC의 구성

- Listening Test ·························· Test 부분은 다음의 4 Part로 나누어진다.
  PART I ······························ Sentences About Photographs(사진 묘사 문제) 6문항
  PART II ······························Stimuli-Responses(응답 문제) 25문항
  PART III ······························ Short Conversations(회화 문제) 39문항

PART IV ··· Short Talks^(설명문 문제) 30문항

■ Reading Test ································· Test 부분은 3 Part로 구성되어 있다.
PART V ························· Sentence Completion^(문장구조 문법·어휘 문제) 30문항
PART VI ·························Passage Completion^(문단완성 문제) 16문항
PART VII ························· Reading Comprehension^(독해 문제) 54문항

실제 시험 시간은 Listening Test에 45분, Reading Test에 75분이 배분된다.

③ TOEIC의 평가 기준

수준	TOEIC	평 가
A	860점 이상	Non-Native로서 충분한 커뮤니케이션을 할 수 있다. 자기가 경험한 범위 내에서는 전문 분야 이외의 화제에 대해서도 충분한 이해와 적절한 표현을 할 수 있다. Native Speaker의 경지에는 다소 못 미친다할지라도 어휘, 문법, 구문의 어느 것이든 정확히 파악하고, 유창하게 구사할 수 있는 능력을 갖고 있다.
B	860~730점	어떠한 상황에서도 적절한 커뮤니케이션을 할 수 있는 소지를 갖추고 있다. 보통 회화는 완전히 이해하고, 응답도 빠르다. 화제가 특수 분야에 미치더라도 대응할 수 있는 능력을 지니고 있다. 업무상으로도 큰 지장이 없다. 정확하냐 하는 점과, 유창하냐 하는 점에는 개인차가 있으며, 문법 구문 상의 오류가 발견되는 일도 있으나, 의사소통을 방해할 정도는 아니다.
C	729~470점	일상생활에 필요한 것을 충족하고, 한정된 범위 내에서는 업무상의 커뮤니케이션을 할 수 있다. 보통 회화라면 요점을 이해하고, 응답에도 지장이 없다. 복잡한 경우에 있어서의 적절한 대응이나 의사 소통은 사람에 따라서 잘하고 못하는 차이가 있다. 기본적인 문법 구문을 익히고 있으며, 표현력은 부족하나마 일단은 자기의 의사를 전달하는 어휘력을 갖추고 있다.

수준	TOEIC	평 가
D	469~220점	보통 회화에서 최소한의 커뮤니케이션을 할 수 있다. 천천히 말해 주거나, 되풀이 또는 딴 말로 바꾸어 말해 주면, 간단한 회화는 이해할 수 있다. 친숙한 화제라면 응답도 가능하다. 어휘, 문법, 구문이 모두 불충분한 점이 많으나, 상대가 Non-Native에게 특별한 배려를 해주는 경우에는 의사소통이 될 수 있다.
E	220점 이하	커뮤니케이션을 할 수 있는 단계에 이르지 못했다. 단순히 회화를 천천히 말해도 부분적으로 이해 못한다. 단편적으로 단어를 늘어놓을 뿐, 실질적으로 의사소통에는 도움을 못 준다.

4 10 Tips for the Test

1. Keep careful track of time.

2. Don't read the directions or look at the sample questions.

3. Answer the easy questions first and then tackle down the hard ones.

4. Be aware of the difficulty of each question.

5. If you are not sure of an answer, guess if you can eliminate even one of the choices.

6. Fill in the answers on your answer sheet in blocks.

7. Answer the questions based only on the informations provided — never on what you think you already know.

8. Don't change answers capriciously on a last minute hunch or whim, or for fear there have been too many A's or not enough B's, in such cases more often than not, students change right answers to wrong ones.

9. Don't bogged down on any one question, and don't rush.

10. Remember that you don't have to answer every question to do well.

Contents

Contents

TOEIC Extended

TOEIC Extended

PART
01

문장 편

CHAPTER
01

CHAPTER 01

단문

문장^(=단문)은 **주어**와 **술어**로 구성된다. **주어**는 **문장**의 **주인**이고, 주체이다. **술어**는 **주어**를 서술하거나, **설명**하는 **말**이다.

1 주어

주어는 **명사, 대명사, 명사구, 명사절**로 이루어진다. 주어를 해석할 때 '−은, −는, −가, −이'를 붙인다.

1) 명사

The hotel has a good reputation.
그 호텔은 명성이 좋다.

2) 대명사

He was hired by the hotel.
그는 그 호텔에 고용되었다.

3) 명사구

To take care of customers is his job.
고객 돌보는 것이 그의 일이다.

4) 명사절

That he transferred to a local branch is surprising.
그가 지방 지점으로 옮겼다는 것은 놀랍다.

실전문제

01 _____ are required to attend the year-end ceremony
which will be held at the Conference Room in the main building.

(A) Employees   (B) Employee   (C) To employing   (D) Employ

02 If the board decided to computerize our management systems,
_____ will have a significant effect on our work.

(A) it   (B) we   (C) they   (D) you

03 _____ on the launch in the rain caused him to catch
a cold, so he called in sick to his company.

(A) Working   (B) Work   (C) Workable   (D) Worked

04 To be left alive in this company, it is true _____ service
is the most important thing, since service gets more customers.

(A) what   (B) or   (C) and   (D) that

2 술어

술어는 **동사, 목적어, 보어**로 구성된다.

1) 동사

동사는 뒤에 목적어나 보어가 어떻게 오느냐에 따라서 다음 **5가지**로 나눈다.

(1) 1형식동사 : 동사 뒤에 **아무 것도 오지 않고**, '주어가 동사하다'로 해석한다.

The delegation to headquarters has **come**.
본사 방문단이 돌아왔다.

The new employee **lives** in Incheon.
새 직원은 인천에 산다.

The manager still **smokes**.
매니저는 아직도 담배를 피운다.

There **are** many checks before launching.
출시 전에는 체크 할게 많다.

It **seems** that my supervisor is diligent.
내 상사는 매우 근면하다.

1형식동사 예 : come(오다), live(살다), smoke(담배를 피우다), be(있다), seem(-라
고 생각되다), go(가다), arrive(도착하다), count(중요하다), die(죽다),
fly(날다)

실전문제

05 It _____ that there is a little chance of a settlement of the negotiation between the management and the union.

(A) seems   (B) gives   (C) offers   (D) becomes

06 When you _____ college next year you will have to decide whether to continue your studies or seek employment.

(A) graduate from   (B) graduate

(C) go   (D) goes

07 You will be considered when there _____ a vacancy in our hotel, but we can't guarantee anything as of now.

(A) smells   (B) loves   (C) is   (D) consider

08 The lecturer at the Cultural Center _____ about the Maori music and art of New Zealand.

(A) told   (B) discussed   (C) talked   (D) mentioned

(2) **2형식동사** : **동사**와 **주격보어**로 구성되고, '주어가 보어가 되다'나, '주어가 보어 상태로 되다'로 해석한다.

The employee **looks** tired.
직원이 피곤해 보인다.

The graduate **became** a hotelier.
졸업생이 호텔리어가 되었다.

The assistant manager still **remains** single.
대리님은 아직도 독신이다.

The president words always **sounds** interesting.
사장님의 말씀은 항상 재미있다.

The applicant's qualifications **are** very impressive.
그 지원자의 자격요건은 끝내준다.

2형식동사 예 : be(-이다), become(-이 되다), turn(-한 상태가 되다), remain(-인 상태로 남다), look(-처럼 보이다), taste(-한 맛이 나다), smell(-한 냄새가 나다), sound(-처럼 들리다), fee(-처럼 느끼다)

실전문제

09 When we are not too _____ about our salary, but devote ourselves to our job, then success comes of itself.

(A) anxiety　　(B) anxiously　　(C) anxious　　(D) anger

10 The food of the restaurant smells so _____ that the team leader highly recommends it to his team members.

(A) deliciousity　(B) deliciousness　(C) deliciously　(D) delicious

11 It is strictly prohibited to mail through parcel post any merchandise that might prove _____ in transport.

(A) dangerous　(B) danger　　(C) dangerously　(D) endanger

12 The old manager in my department insists on remaining _____ till she has her own house and an apartment.

(A) single　　(B) singleness　(C) singular　(D) singly

(3) **3형식동사** : **동사**와 **목적어**로 구성되고, '주어가 목적어를 동사하다'로 해석한다.

The inspector **found** a problem.
검사관은 문제를 하나 발견했다.

The staff **finished** loading the products onto the truck.
직원들은 제품을 트럭에 싣기를 끝냈다.

They **say** that the Korean economy is not good.
사람들은 한국 경제가 좋지 않다고들 말한다.

The employee **read** the manual several times.
직원은 매뉴얼을 여러 차례 읽었다.

The team members **want** to be loved by the manager.
팀원들은 팀장의 사랑을 받기를 원한다.

3형식동사 예 : find(-을 찾다), forget(-을 잊다), finish(-을 끝내다), believe(-을 믿다),
read(-을 읽다), want(-을 원하다), enjoy(-을 즐기다), wish(-을 소원하
다), call on(-을 방문하다), call up(-에게 전화를 걸다)

 ## 실전문제

13 The employee _____ his departure of the urgent business
trip until morning, for he was tired and afraid to drive at night.

(A) put   (B) began   (C) delayed   (D) gave

14 The most successful business man _____ to me that the
most important factor in any business is not money but service.

(A) says   (B) tells   (C) talks   (D) speaks

15 The new arrangement of machines on the factory floor _____
a number of advantages over the old arrangement.

(A) is   (B) takes   (C) makes   (D) has

16 This position _____ a lot of flexibility and least five
years' experience in the tourist industry.

(A) requires   (B) provides   (C) applies   (D) acquires

(4) **4형식동사** : **동사**와 **간접 목적어, 직접 목적어**로 구성 된다. **간접 목적어**로는
사람이 나오고, **직접 목적어**로는 **사물**이 나온다. '주어가 간접목적어(=사람)

에게 직접목적어(=사물)를 동사하다'로 해석한다.

The manager **gave** his staff some instructions.
매니저는 직원들에게 지시사항을 하달했다.

He **showed** the guard his ID card.
그는 경비원에게 자신의 신분증을 보여주었다.

The team manager **told** the team members his job.
팀장님은 팀원들에게 자기의 역할을 말했다.

My team leader **bought** me a birthday cake.
팀장님께서 내게 생일 케익을 하나 사주셨다.

4형식동사 예 : give(A에게 B를 주다), offer(A에게 B를 주다), tell(A에게 B를 말하다), show(A에게 B를 보여주다), bring(A에게 B를 가져다주다), teach(A에게 B를 가르쳐주다), buy(A에게 B를 사주다), send(A에게 B를 보내주다), grant(A에게 B를 허락하다)

실전문제

17 Deluxe hotels will _____ you much better service than other ordinary hotels even though they are expensive.

   (A) offer   (B) take   (C) show   (D) provide

18 Since Costco is the cheapest supplier nearby, it won't _____ to shop around for better prices instead of Costco.

   (A) do us well   (B) do us good   (C) be well us   (D) do good us

19 A licensed computer program will include complete instructions that _____ users how they operate the program.

(A) say (B) tell (C) speak (D) talk

20 When I _____ him what day he could send the promotional material, he said he was not positive himself.

(A) said (B) asked (C) took (D) provided

(5) **5형식동사** : **동사**와 **목적어, 목적보어**로 구성되고, '주어는 목적어가 목적보어 하도록 동사하다'로 해석된다.

All the employees **elected** him the union leader.
모든 직원은 그를 노조 지부장으로 뽑았다.

The company **consider**s the launch successful.
회사는 그 (신제품) 출시가 성공적이라고 생각한다.

All staff **named** her their project leader.
모든 직원은 그녀를 프로젝트의 장으로 선출했다.

My supervisor **made** us work overtime.
내 상사는 우리가 야근 하도록 했다.

The worker **saw** his coworker make a mistake.
그 인부는 동료가 실수하는 것을 목격했다.

5형식동사 예 : find(A를 B라고 생각하다), elect(A를 B로 선출하다), consider(A를 B라고 여기다), appoint(A를 B로 임명하다), think(A를 B라고 생각하다), make(A를 B하게 만들다)

실전문제

21 At first we _____ the team manager to be an opponent of ours, but later we found his opinion to be acceptable.

(A) imagined   (B) implied   (C) wanted   (D) supposed

22 When we consider the worker-owner relationship, it is a natural conclusion that owners want the job _____ done quickly.

(A) is   (B) to be   (C) be   (D) was

23 The team manager had the thrill of seeing sales records _____ by our sales team twice in a year.

(A) broken   (B) to break   (C) be broken (D) to be broken

24 He refused to let this colleagues _____ the file as there was a lot of confidential information in it.

(A) see   (B) seeing   (C) to see   (D) to have seen

2) 목적어

목적어는 동사 뒤에 위치하는, **동사**의 **행위**나 **상태**가 **가해지는 대상**을 말하며, 주어처럼 **명사, 대명사, 명사구, 명사절**(=명사)이 목적어가 된다.

(1) 목적어가 1개인 경우 : 3형식 동사가 하나의 목적어를 취한다.

명사 : The new equipment improved **efficiency** by 30 percent.
새 장비는 효율을 30% 정도 개선시켰다.

대명사 : I found **it** on the conveyer belt.
운반 벨트에서 그 것을 찾았다.

명사구: We finally finished **loading the boxes onto the truck.**
우리는 마침내 트럭에 박스 싣기를 끝냈다.

명사절: We think **that the new booking system is efficient.**
우리는 그 새 예약 시스템이 효율적이라고 생각한다.

(2) **목적어가 2개인 경우** : **4형식 동사**가 두개의 목적어(간접목적어+직접목적어)를 취한다.

Guests should show **the attendant invitations** at the entrance.
손님들은 입구에서 관리인에게 초청장을 보여줘야 한다.

The manager gave **me the instructions.**
팀장님은 내게 지시사항을 하달하셨다.

The manager told **me an idea.**
팀장님은 내게 그 아이디어를 말씀하셨다.

The company will send **you an application for the position.**
회사는 그 자리에 대한 지원서를 당신에게 보낼 겁니다.

 실전문제

25 The Small and Midium Industry Bank completed _____ of the new building for its headquarters after three years.

(A) construct (B) construction
(C) constructing (D) to construct

26 Korea Telecommunication provides _____ with the customers who regularly use long-distance calls oversees.

(A) to discount (B) discount
(C) discounts (D) discounting

27   After the assistant manager passed the after-managerial course test, the marketing manager gave her more _____.

     (A) responsibility   (B) respond

     (C) responsible   (D) responsibly

28   I asked the personnel department to send _____ an application form for the vacant position by the end of this week.

     (A) you   (B) your   (C) yours   (D) yourself

3) 보어

주어를 서술하면 **주격 보어**라 하고, **목적어**를 서술하면 **목적격 보어**라 한다.

(1) 주격 보어

2형식 동사 뒤에서 앞의 **주어를 서술**한다.

His qualifications are **impressive**.
그의 자격요건은 끝내준다

The employee became **an assistant manager** soon.
그 직원은 곧 대리가 되었다.

The employee looks very **tired** now.
직원은 지금 몹시 피곤해 보인다.

The production level remained **stable**.
생산 수준은 여전히 안정된 상태이다.

(2) 목적격 보어

5형식 동사의 목적어 뒤에서 앞의 **목적어를 서술**한다.

The manager found the measures **necessary**.
팀장님은 그 조치들이 필요하다 고 생각한다.

All members elected him **director of the project**.
모든 팀원들은 그를 프로젝트의 책임자로 선출했다.

We consider the project **profitable**.
우리는 그 프로젝트가 이익을 준다고 여기고 있다.

 ## 실전문제

29 The director became more _____ after he had retired from the Samsung Electronics after thirty years of service.

    (A) popularize   (B) popularly
    (C) popular   (D) popularity

30 The board of directors elected him _____ of the board of directors at the annual shareholders meeting.

    (A) famous   (B) choose
    (C) chairman   (D) popularly

31 The company convention hall's decorations are very attractive but the lightening inside the hall is too _____.

    (A) dim   (B) dims
    (C) dimly   (D) dimness

32 The online resources which our company provides with clients make free information _____ to all users.

    (A) accessibly   (B) accessible
    (C) access   (D) accessibility

3 제조 어휘 연구

1) **equipment** n. 장비, 설비; v. **equip** 장비를 갖추다

   ex: 등산장비를 챙기다.

2) **supervision** n. 감독, 관리; v. **supervise** 감독하다

   ex: 현장을 감독하다.

3) **manufacture** v. 제조하다; n. **manufacturing** 제조, 제조업

   ex: 상품을 제조하다.

4) **inspector** n. 검사관; v. **inspect** 검사하다, 조사하다

   ex: 공장 기계를 검사하다.

5) **product** n. 제품; v. **produce** 생산하다

   ex: 제품을 생산하다.

6) **instructions** n. (사용) 설명서; v. **instruct** 설명하다, 지시하다

   ex: 사용설명서를 먼저 읽으세요.

실전문제

33 If your _____ is unavailable, report to the security officer, or go to the personnel department.

(A) popularity　　　　　(B) inspection
(C) equipment　　　　　(D) instructions

34 Our major export goods are clothes which have been tested as thoroughly as any _____ has ever been tested.

(A) product   (B) equipment   (C) works   (D) produce

4 독해 연구

Art Exhibition

Meet more than 100 artists and see the work of painters, sculptors, photographers, and designers at the Art Exhibition this Saturday and Sunday. The historic twelve-building complex, formerly the Textile Factory, is now home to hundreds of artists who will open their studies to the public. Noted local photographer Hashimoto gives talks at 1 p.m. both days. Tours of the buildings start at noon on Saturday only.

Art Exhibition is open on Saturday, from 10 a.m. to 7 p.m., and Sunday, 11 a.m. to 6 p.m. It's located on Main Street at Route 40 near downtown. There is no admission fee. Art and refreshments are for sale. Parking fee is $2. Telephone number is (415) 555-4397.

 실전문제

35 What is the best title for this notice?

(A) "Historic Tour Scheduled"   (B) "Weekend Walkathon"
(C) "Hashimoto to Lecture"   (D) "Two-Day Art Display"

36   The Art Exhibition offers all of the following EXCEPT.

    (A) art exhibits.

    (B) walks through historic buildings.

    (C) sculpture classes.

    (D) lectures on photography

37   What is the historic Factory used for?

    (A) Artists' studios

    (B) A drama theater

    (C) A manufacturing center

    (D) An athletic club

38   What does the word 'complex' mean?

    (A) scheme

    (B) structure

    (C) network

    (D) organization

T O E I C Extended

CHAPTER
02

중문

단문 두 개가 **등위 접속사**로 **연결**된 **문장**을 **중문**이라 한다. 등위 접속사에는 **완전 등위 접 속사, 준 등위 접속사, 등위 상관 접속사**가 있다.

1 완전 등위 접속사

접속된 **두 문장**이 **대등**하다 해서 **완전 등위 접속사**라 부르며, 아래 세 가지가 있다.

1) **And** : 그리고, 그리고 나서, 그래서

My colleague said good-bye, **and** went out.
내 동료는 안녕이라고 말하고는 나가버렸다.

My manager is secretive **and** your manager is candid.
내 팀장님은 비밀스럽지만 네 팀장님은 솔직하다.

2) **But** : 그러나, 그럼에도 불구하고,

The president is very rich **but** not happy.
회장님은 부자이시나 행복하지가 않다.

I love the company **but** the company doesn't love me.
나는 나의 회사를 사랑하지만 회사는 나를 사랑하지 않는다.

3) Or : 또는, 그렇지 않으면

He went to work **or** was at home.
그는 직장에 갔거나 아니면 집에 있었을 것이다

My president is interested in gambling **or** sports.
내 회장님은 도박이나 스포츠에 흥미가 있다.

실전문제

01 We must leave the lunch table before 1:00 _____ we will be late for afternoon president meeting.

  (A) for   (B) or   (C) and   (D) but

02 My supervisor has been looking over the annual report all day long, _____ he has discovered no error so far.

  (A) and   (B) but   (C) or   (D) for

03 Something unavoidable must have happened to the supervisor who usually arrives on time, _____ he would have been here now.

  (A) and   (B) or   (C) so   (D) so that

04 Our company attorney handles taxes and estates very well, _____ he's also quite good at accounting.

  (A) and   (B) but   (C) for   (D) or

2 준 등위 접속사

접속된 두 개의 문장이 **대등**하지 **않아서 준 등위 접속사**라 한다.

1) For : 왜냐하면(=굳이 이유를 들자면)

I didn't worked overtime, **for** I was tired very much.
나는 야근을 하지 않았다, 굳이 이유를 대자면 매우 피곤했기 때문이다.

I just did it, **for** my manager ask me to do it.
굳이 이유를 대자면 팀장님이 내게 그 것을 하라 해서 했을 뿐이다.

2) As well as : 뿐만 아니라

My boss has experience **as well as** knowledge.
내 상사는 지식 뿐 아니라 경험도 가지고 있다.

You **as well as** he are to blame for the bas sales record.
그 뿐만 아니라 너도 저조한 판매 실적에 비난을 받아야 한다.

3) So : 그래서

It was still painful **so** I went to see a doctor.
아직도 아파서 의사를 보러갔다.

3 등위 상관 접속사

접속된 두 개의 문장이 **대등** 할 뿐 아니라 접속사도 두 개가 **서로 관계**(=상관)가 있다 해서 **등위 상관 접속사**라 부른다.

1) both A and B : A, B 둘 다; not only A but also B : A 뿐 아니라 B도

Sales of our products have improved **both** locally **and** nationally.
우리 제품의 판매량은 전국적으로 늘었다.

The spa provides **not only** full-body massages, **but also** skin treatments.
그 온천은 전신 마사지는 물론 피부 치료도 해준다.

2) **either A or B** : A나 B 둘 중 하나; **not A but B** : A가 아니라 B

The club meets in **either** the lounge **or** the cafeteria.
그 클럽은 휴게실 아니면 구내식당에서 만난다.

She is **not** a hotelier **but** a duty-free shop clerk.
그녀는 호텔리어가 아니고 면세점 직원이다.

3) **neither A nor B** : A나 B 둘 다 아닌

Some clients **neither** completed the survey **nor** submitted it.
일부 고객들은 설문지를 작성하지도 않았을 뿐만 아니라 제출도 하지 않았다.

 ## 실전문제

05 The employee delayed his departure until tomorrow morning, _____ he was tired and afraid to drive at night.

 (A) for   (B) when   (C) and   (D) or

06 _____ late for the afternoon meeting but he also arrived drunk let alone a report for his business trip.

 (A) He was   (B) Not only was he
 (C) Neither was he   (D) Both he was

07 I do not regard the matter as an either choice, but the team leader ordered either you _____ she to go.

 (A) and   (B) but   (C) or   (D) nor

08 _____ the President and the Vice-President will
appear on national television to answer questions about the
operation.

(A) Either   (B) Both   (C) So   (D) Not only

4 제품 어휘 연구

1) **release** v. 출시하다; s. launch
   ex: 새 상품을 출시하다.

2) **feature** v. 특색 있게 다루다; n. 특징, 특색
   ex: 그 사건을 다루다.

3) **ship** v. 배송하다; n. 배송; s. deliver
   ex: 집으로 배송 시키다.

4) **distribution** n. 유통; v. **distribute** 유통시키다
   ex: 불법적으로 유통시키다.

5) **order** n. 주문, 주문품; v. 주문하다
   ex: 물건을 주문하다.

6) **transaction** n. 거래; v. **transact** 거래하다
   ex: 거래를 성사시키다.

실전문제

09   The sunken living rooms are a unique _____ of our hotel which is designed by a world-famous architect.

    (A) transaction   (B) distribution
    (C) feature   (D) manual

10   The companies which we are competing with for the _____ did not disclose terms of the transaction so far.

    (A) feature   (B) distribution
    (C) ship   (D) order

5 독해 연구

Regent Hotels and Resorts

For the business traveler whose needs reach far beyond the in-room coffee maker, we introduce the Regent Corporate Club Room, a work space cleverly disguised as sleeping quarters.

With a swivel desk chair, a fax/printer/copier, and a desk lamp with outlets for your laptop, you'll be able to carry out the corporate mission in total comfort. And because we offer the Internet service, you can use your laptop to keep in touch with your business partners.

To request a Regent Corporate Club Room for your next stay, call your travel agent or 1-800-555-3586. For on-line reservations visit us at www.regent.com.

실전문제

11 Who is the audience for this advertisement?

(A) Telephone service providers   (B) Business Travelers
(C) Families with children   (D) Hotel workers

12 Which of the following is NOT provided by the hotel?

(A) A desk   (B) A fax machine
(C) A coffee maker   (D) A laptop computer

13 What is being offered in this ad?

(A) Hotel office space   (B) A modified hotel room
(C) Conference facilities   (D) A phone card

14 What does the word 'quarters' mean?

(A) districts   (B) rooms
(C) places   (D) regions

복문

하나의 단문 밑에 또 하나의 단문이 **종속적**으로 **연결된 문장**을 **복문**이라고 한다. 종속된 문장이 **명사** 자리에 오면 **명사절**, **형용사** 자리에 오면 **형용사절**, **부사** 자리에 오면 **부사절**이라 한다.

1 명사절

명사절에는 **접속사절, 의문사절, 자유 관계사절**이 있다.

1) 접속사절

(1) That 절

100% 단정적인 내용을 이끌 때 쓴다.

That the world is round is obvious.
지구가 둥글다는 사실은 자명하다.

I know **that** the Korean economy is not so good.
한국 경제가 썩 좋지 않다는 것을 안다.

실전문제

01 The management decided _____ we couldn't reduce the price any further, since we couldn't sell the new goods below cost.

(A) what   (B) that   (C) whether   (D) if

02 Please be assured _____ your application form has been received and you will be notified of the interview schedule.

(A) what   (B) that   (C) if   (D) whether

(2) If 절

1%-99%까지 그 확실성을 **모르는 내용**을 이끌 때 쓴다.

We should decide **if** we start early tomorrow morning.
우리는 내일 아침 일찍 출발해야 하는가를 결정해야만 한다.

I don't know **if** his first reaction to the salary reduction was yes.
봉급 삭감에 대한 그의 첫 반응이 긍정이었는지 어떤지에 대해서 모른다.

(3) Whether 절

0%이거나 100%인 **내용**을 이끌 때 쓴다.

Whether the oil price will go up or not is unknown.
기름 값이 오를 것인지 아닌지는 알려져 있지 않다.

I don't know **whether** the order will arrive today or not.
그 주문이 오늘 올지 안 올지는 나도 모른다.

27

실전문제

03 Since the general manager didn't know _____ there would be a salary raise or not, he couldn't decide to stay here or not.

(A) if   (B) whether   (C) that   (D) what

04 I don't know _____ my senior staff had helped me before, but I assure you that I will help you at any time you ask me.

(A) that   (B) for   (C) why   (D) if

2) 의문사절

who, when, where, what, how, why가 만드는 **간법 의문문**을 말한다.

How he gets the money is his own affair.
돈은 어떻게 벌 것인가는 순전히 그의 일이다.

I don't know **what** made him do that.
뭐가 그로 하여금 그 것을 하게 했는지는 나도 모른다.

실전문제

05 We often enjoy a hot and refreshing tea in the employee's lounge, but we don't think about _____ tea comes from.

(A) why   (B) when   (C) where   (D) that

06 We want to know _____ you guessed the exact statistic figures you weren't sure about, since accounting is not your major.

(A) which   (B) why   (C) when   (D) how

3) 자유 관계사 절

관계사가 **선행사를 포함**하고 있어서 다른 관계절처럼 **관계절**이 **선행사**에 **매여** 있지 **않다**. 그래서 **자유 관계사 절**이라 부른다.

(1) what/whatever 절

What you have do is put the parts together.(=That which)
당신이 해야 할 것은 부문 품을 조립하는 것이다.

Do **whatever** you would like to do.(=anything that which)
네가 하고 싶은 것을 하라.

(2) 의문사+ever 절

You may take **whichever** you like best.(=anything which)
네가 가장 좋아하는 것을 가져가도 좋다.

I will give it to **whoever** comes first.(=anyone who)
제일 먼저 온 사람에게 그 것을 주겠다.

 실전문제

07 A wise manager will assign a job to _____ is best qualified for the job which requires to computerize the bookkeeping.

(A) what   (B) whoever
(C) whatever   (D) whomever

08 The leader of the project has not the least interest in _____ the team members propose to do.

(A) which   (B) what
(C) when   (D) why

2 형용사절(=관계절)

절이 형용사자리에 온 것으로, 뒤에 있는 절(=관계절)이 **앞의 명사**(=선행사)를 **수식**하는 **절**을 **형용사절**(관계절)이라 한다.

1) 관계절의 종류

(1) 관계 대명사절

관계사가 관계절 안에서 **명사 자리**(=주어, 목적어)를 대신한다.

He is a taxi driver **who** belongs to the company.(=주어)
그는 회사에 소속된 택시 기사다.

The bad weather caused a delay **which** we can't handle with.(=목적어)
나쁜 날씨는 우리도 어쩔 수 없는 지연을 가져왔다.

실전문제

09 Tourism industry is a field of hospitality _____ needs a lot of dedication and commitment from us.

    (A) what   (B) where
    (C) that   (D) which

10 Investors are the most important persons _____ you can depend on for the success of your new business.

    (A) what   (B) that
    (C) whom   (D) which

(2) 관계 형용사절

관계사가 관계절 안에서 **형용사 자리**^(=소유격)를 대신한다.

He met a director **whose** film won the film award.
자기의 영화가 영화상을 탄 감독이다.

There are many workers **whose** salaries are affected by the inflation.
자기들의 월급이 인플레이션에 영향을 받는 노동자들이 많다.

실전문제

11   The number of employees _____ salary is reduced by the company merger and restructuring is more than half.

(A) whose   (B) who   (C) whom   (D) of whom

12   They are good at dealing with customers' complaints, but there are various problems, the solution _____ is helpless.

(A) to which   (B) of them   (C) of which   (D) to them

(3) 관계 부사절

관계사가 관계절 안에서 **부사 자리**^(=장소, 방법, 시간)를 대신한다.

Fall is the season **when** most companies host employee picnics outdoors.
가을은 많은 회사들이 야외로 직원 소풍을 가는 계절이다.

I finally find out the reason **why** the traffic is so heavy.
마침내 교통이 복잡한 이유를 찾아냈다.

This is the company **where** I belong.
이곳이 내가 다니는 회사이다.

실전문제

13 When I asked for some softwares, the shopkeeper went to the factory cupboard _____ many rare software was kept.

(A) which   (B) where   (C) that   (D) there

14 According to what I've experienced, there comes a time _____ he has to think about leaving the company.

(A) where   (B) in which   (C) when   (D) why

2) 관계사의 종류

(1) 사람 관계사

선행사가 **사람**일 때 who를 쓴다.

We have only two airline agents **who** check boarding passes.
우리는 탑승권을 확인하는 항공사직원이 둘 밖에 없다.

I also admire employees **whom** everyone admires.
나 역시 모두가 좋아하는 직원을 좋아한다.

 실전문제

15 Today the number of workers _____ go on strike for higher wages is twice that of a decade ago.

(A) who   (B) which   (C) that   (D) who

16　In the financial world, anyone ＿＿＿＿＿＿ receives business information in advance is in a position to profit from it.

(A) what　　　(B) who　　　(C) whom　　　(D) that

(2) 사물 관계사

선행사가 **사물**일 때 **which**를 쓴다.

I hate the embassy **which** is located in the suburbs.
외곽에 위치한 대사관을 좋아하지 않는다.

There are many problems the solution of **which** is helpless.
해결책이 무기력한 많은 문제들이 존재한다.

실전문제

17　Try to put yourselves in the team member's place and to see why they do the things ＿＿＿＿＿＿ you strongly disagree with.

(A) what　　(B) whom　　(C) who　　(D) which

18　My colleague is good at sales ＿＿＿＿＿＿ I am bad at, so I always fall behind him in annual performance records.

(A) which　　(B) what　　(C) and　　(D) but

(3) 대신 관계사

사람 관계사 **who**나 사물 관계사 **which** 대신에 ^(접속사) **that**을 ^(빌려다) 쓴다.

I made an appointment with him **that** is urgent.
나는 그와 긴급한 약속을 했다

The **back**biting that goes on in that company is awful.
그 회사에서 오가는 험담은 끔찍하다.

실전문제

19 The restructuring which is being carried out is something
_____ should never happen again in this company.

(A) which   (B) who
(C) that   (D) what

20 Thank you again for all _____ your members did
during our stay in your hotel in order to attend the meeting.

(A) what   (B) that
(C) which   (D) whom

3) 관계사의 생략

(1) **관계사+be 생략** : 일반 모든 동사의 경우

The employee **standing** near the window is my manager.(=who is standing)
창가에 서있는 직원이 내 팀장이다.

(2) **관계사+-s 생략+-ing** : want, wish, love, stop 등과 같은 **상태**나 **순간 동사**의 경우

The employee **wishing** to transfer is just my colleague.(=who wishes)
전근을 희망하는 직원이 바로 내 동료다.

21 Banks make most of their income from interest _____ on loans and investments in stocks and bonds.

(A) earning   (B) earned   (C) which earned   (D) that earned

22 It is important for income seekers and it is important for people _____ to grow their portfolio over time.

(A) wants   (B) wanting   (C) to want   (D) wanted

❸ 부사절

문장에서 동사의 행위나 상태가 일어나는 **장소, 방법, 시간**을 나타내는 절이다.

1) 장소절

We camped **where** there was enough water.(=at the place where)
우리는 충분한 물이 있는 곳에서 캠핑을 했다.

You can camp **wherever** people had camped.(=at any place where)
우리는 사람들이 캠핑했던 곳이면 어디든지 캠핑을 할 수 있다.

 실전문제

23 Our new corporate headquarters was built _____ there had once been the city hall before.

(A) in which   (B) where   (C) on which   (D) in where

24   The computer repair technician travels to provide technical

support _____ his customers are waiting for him.

(A) the place   (B) why   (C) when   (D) where

2) 방법절

장소절과 **시간절**을 **제외**한 모든 **절**을 말한다.

(1) 조건절

If the hotel allows the fruit, I can carry it to the hotel.
호텔이 그 과일을 허락한다면 그 과일을 호텔로 들여갈 수 있다.

Unless the goods are on sale, we cannot afford it.
그 상품이 세일중이 아니라면 우리는 그 것을 살 수가 없다.

(2) 양보절

Though our manager is not intelligent, he is candid.
우리 팀장님이 현명하지는 않지만 솔직하다.

Even though I visited many places, I didn't buy any souvenirs.
많은 곳을 방문했지만 어떤 기념품도 사지 않았다.

(3) 이유절

Because the goods are defective, he asked for a refund.
그 상품들이 결함이 있어서 그는 환불을 요구했다.

Since he doesn't have much money, he can't buy a BMW.
그는 돈이 많지 않아서 BMW를 살 수 없었다.

As the exchange rate was favorable, I exchanged much money.
환율이 좋아서 돈을 많이 바꿨다.

실전문제

25 The theater manager told me not to let anybody in except for authorized people _____ he shows his valid ticket.

(A) if   (B) unless   (C) though   (D) provided

26 The victims of the building collapse were taken to the hospital _____ they had been wounded seriously on the spot.

(A) which   (B) because   (C) that   (D) though

27 _____ we completed the contract, we could not forget the hard negotiation process with the counter party.

(A) Though   (B) However   (C) As   (D) If

(4) 목적절

Speak a little louder **so that** we can all hear you.
우리 모두가 당신 말을 들을 수 있도록 좀 더 크게 말하세요.

She visited her home town **in order that** he could see her parents.
부모님 보러 시골을 방문했다.

(5) 결과절

He was **so** late **that** he miss the bus.
그는 너무 늦어 셔틀버스를 놓쳤다.

It was a **such** a good weather **that** we had a launching outside.
날씨가 너무 좋아서 우리 회사는 출시회를 밖에서 했다.

실전문제

28 Since employment training is a necessary programme, it should be organized _____ none of the talks overlaps.

(A) so that　　(B) in that　　(C) such that　　(D) in order to

29 Ms. Lee did _____ good work on that project that she was quickly offered a promotion.

(A) too　　(B) such　　(C) so　　(D) much

3) 시간절

(1) **When**(-할 때, -하면), **As**(-하면서, -할 때), **While**(-하는 동안에)

I was handsome **when** I was young.
나도 젊었을 때는 잘 생겼었다.

The employee sang softly **as** he worked.
직원은 일하면서 나직하게 노래했다.

While I was trying on clothes, my colleagues waited outside.
내가 옷을 입어 보는 동안 동료들은 밖에서 기다렸다.

(2) **Before**(-전에), **After**(-후에), **Until**(-까지)

I couldn't finish the work **before** the manager came back.
팀장님께서 돌아오시기 전에 그 일을 끝낼 수 없었다.

I will go back to my country **after** I finish my work.
일 끝나면 귀국할 것이다.

(3) **Since**(-이래로), **As soon as**(-하자마자)

Nothing has happened so far **since** we departed yesterday.
어제 우리가 헤어진 이후 지금까지 아무 일도 일어나지 않았습니다.

I will let you know **as soon as** the assistant manager arrives.
대리님이 오시는 대로 알려드리겠습니다.

실전문제

30 _____ I get the interview result for the managerial position, I'll call you in a hurry or I'll send it by e-mail.

(A) Not sooner than   (B) No sooner
(C) So soon than   (D) As soon as

31 Even though the product is developed completely, there could be additional steps to proceed even _____ we launch it into the market.

(A) when   (B) since   (C) after   (D) before

32 We should think about every possible danger we cannot fully predict _____ we start a new business.

(A) by   (B) until   (C) when   (D) since

33 The striking workers say that they will not return to their jobs _____ they get raises and better working conditions.

(A) since   (B) during   (C) over   (D) until

4 제조 어휘 연구

1) **introduce** v. 출시하다, 소개하다; n. **introduction** 출시; s. launch
   ex: 새 상품을 출시하다.

39

2) **streamline** v. 간소화하다, 유선형으로 하다; s. simplify

   ex: 서류 업무를 간소화 시키다.

3) **fragile** a. 깨지기 쉬운; s. delicate

   ex: 깨지기 쉬운 물건 안 받는다.

4) **transport** v. 운송하다; n. **transportation** 운송

   ex: 물품을 운송하다.

5) **technician** n. 기술자; a. **technical** 기술적인

   ex: 컴퓨터 기술자를 부르다.

6) **effective** a. 효과적인; ad. **effectively** 효과적으로

   ex: 효과적인 방법을 찾다.

실전문제

34 According to the Mail Transport Act _____ items should be carefully packaged to avoid shipping damage.

  (A) broken   (B) fragile
  (C) weak   (D) produce

35 The information technology department took a very _____ measure to prevent computer viruses.

  (A) overwhelming   (B) sensational
  (C) better   (D) effective

5 독해 연구

SAS Load Factor

With increasing Korean travelers visiting Scandinavia, SAS's Korean-Scandinavia North Pole route made the highest load factor of 78.7 percent during the 2015-2016 financial year, said Mogens K. Rasmussen, SAS general manager for Korea.

The actual number of passengers carried by SAS during 2016 financial year was 8,413,000-up by 20,000. "In the first two months of the new 2017 financial year, SAS passenger traffic has already increased 4 to 5 percent on European routes," he explained. "Systemwide load factor for the new financial year is expected to rise about 10 percent to over 60 percent," he said.

The best passenger traffic gains were on South American and African routes, all increasing more than 20 percent in terms of revenue.

 실전문제

36 During 2016 the number of passengers increased by?

(A) 200,000   (B) 20,000   (C) 8.413.000   (D) 40.000

37 The best passenger traffic was?

(A) South American Routers
(B) African Routes
(C) European Routes
(D) African and South American Routes

38 During 2015-2016 the load factor was?

(A) 74.7%   (B) 78.7%   (C) 80%   (D) 87.7%

TOEIC Extended

TOEIC Extended

PART
02

품사 편

CHAPTER 04

명사

1 한정사

명사 앞에 **명사**와 **1:1로 대응**해 등장하여 뒤의 **명사**를 **한정**하는 것을 **한정사**라 한다.

이러한 한정사에는 **소유형용사, 지시형용사, 수량형용사, 관사** 등이 있다.

1) 소유형용사

my(나의), his(그의), theirs(그들의) 같이 명사 앞에서 그 명사의 **소유자를 나타내는 형용사**를 말한다.

> **My** manager checked the inventory closely.
> 내 팀장님은 물품 목록을 꼼꼼하게 살펴보셨다.

> The employees are having **their** break time.
> 직원들은 그들의 쉬는 시간을 갖고 있는 중이다.

2) 지시형용사

this(these), that(those) 같이 명사 앞에서 그 **명사를 지시하는 형용사**를 말한다.

> **This** package arrived by courier just before.
> 이 소포는 배달원에 의해 방금 전에 도착했다.

> **Those** cell phones are yours.
> 저 핸드폰들이 니들 것이다.

실전문제

01 Being cautious did not pay on _____ occasion, there can be no doubt that this merger is our only choice.

(A) my
(B) your
(C) this
(D) its

02 A good businessman learns more from _____ business opponents than from supporters who flatter people to gain their trust.

(A) their
(B) its
(C) his
(D) her

03 The general affairs department is responsible for supplying office supplies that every company office requires for _____ operation.

(A) its
(B) their
(C) their
(D) its

04 We ask that you should look into the matter since we don't currently have _____ information on the matter of merger.

(A) its
(B) that
(C) our
(D) your

3) 수량형용사

명사 앞에서 그 **명사**의 **수**나 **양**을 나타내는 **형용사**로, 명사가 셀 수 있는 명사냐, 셀 수 없는 명사냐에 따라 다르다.

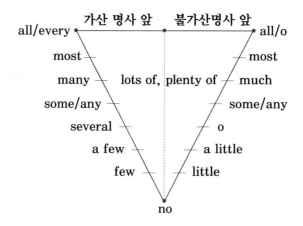

All employees are attended.
모든 직원들이 참석했다.

All coffee is served.
모든 커피가 준비 되었다.

Every employee is attended.
모든 직원이 참석했다.

※ **Every** coffee is served.(※는 비 법적인 문장을 나타낸다.)
　모든 커피가 준비 되었다.

Several workers already went home.
몇몇 노동자들은 벌써 귀가 했다

※ **Several** machinery is prepared.
　몇 개의 기계가 준비가 되었다.

No employees is to leave the office.
어떤 직원도 사무실을 떠날 수 없다.

There are **no** documents on the manager's desk.
매니저의 책상 위에는 어떤 서류도 없다.

실전문제

05 The politician made a fortune in the grocery business, so he already had _____ money before going into politics.

(A) many   (B) lot of   (C) plenty   (D) much

06 _____ are required to attend the year-end ceremony which will be held in the president's residence.

(A) All staff   (B) Every staff   (C) My staffs   (D) All staffs

07 Very _____ people are allowed to get into the research department unless they work for the company.

(A) few   (B) less   (C) much   (D) little

08 Ms. May decided to go to Hong Kong _____ days before the conference started.

(A) several   (B) few   (C) couple   (D) any

4) 관사

a나 the같은 것들을 **관사**라고 하며, **안 정해진 명사 앞에는** a를, **정해진 명사 앞에는** the를 쓴다.

(1) 부정관사

부정관사 **a는 정해지지 않은, 불특정한 하나**를 나타내는 **명사 앞**에 온다.

I have an interview with **an** applicant.
한 지원자와 인터뷰가 있다.

47

There was **a** good lecture in the meeting.
모임 중에 아주 좋은 강연이 하나 있었다.

(2) 정관사

정관사 **the**는 **정해진 명사 앞**에 온다.

We have accepted **the** invitation to the president's birthday party.
우리들은 회장님의 생일파티 초대를 받아 들였다.

The inspector inspects **the** machinery in our factory every month.
검사관은 공장안의 기계들을 매달 검사한다.

 실전문제

09 Steve Jobs is considered one of the most influential new entrepreneur, marketer, and inventor of _____ century.

(A) the 21   (B) 21th   (C) a 21   (D) the 21th

10 If I went to _____ again I would major something useful like business management and business administration.

(A) the college   (B) a college   (C) colleges   (D) college

11 To celebrate the 20th anniversary of the company, the president invited all the employees and we _____ dinner together.

(A) had a   (B) had the   (C) had   (D) had very good

12 Each year tourists from all over the country travel to the village to visit _____ of Steve Jobs.

(A) a birthplace   (B) the birthplace
(C) a birth place   (D) the birth place

2 명사

사물의 **이름**을 지칭하는 말이다. 영어에서는 명사를 **셀 수 있느냐**(=가산명사), **셀 수 없느냐**(=불가산명사)로 나누어 표시한다.

1) 가산명사

하나, 둘 이렇게 **셀 수 있는 명사**를 **가산명사**라고 부른다. **하나** 앞에는 **a**를, **둘 이상** 인 경우는 명사 뒤에 **-s**를 붙인다.

Coffee **prices** are different regionally.
커피 값은 지역적으로 다 다르다.

Refunds are available in this shop.
이 가게에서는 환불이 가능합니다.

The company has two job **openings**.
그 회사는 두 개의 빈자리가 있다.

We need three parking **permits**.
우리 세장의 주차 허가증이 필요하다.

The coffee shop needs three more coffee **machines**.
그 커피숍은 세 개의 기계가 더 필요하다.

명사 예 : price(가격), refund(환불), opening(공석), permit(허가증), machine(기계),
location(장소), result(결과), estimate(견적서), circumstance(상황)

 실전문제

13 The customer service representative has shown me _____,
so that I want to pay her back what little I can.

(A) many kindness (B) many kindnesses
(C) much kindness (D) much kindnesses

14   According to the Economic Affairs, the economy of Korea expanded at ＿＿＿＿＿＿ in the fourth quarter.

(A) the 3.5% rates   (B) the 3.5% rate
(C) 3.5% rates   (D) a 3.5% rate

15   Bank tellers are given the ＿＿＿＿＿＿ of ensuring that all transactions involving money going into and out of an account are accurate.

(A) responses   (B) response
(C) responsibilities   (D) responsibility

16   A large number of ＿＿＿＿＿＿ at this factory are immigrants from the East Asia, most of whom are illegal immigrants.

(A) employee   (B) employments
(C) employment   (D) employees

2) 불가산 명사

하나, 둘 **셀 수 없는 명사**를 불가산 명사라 부르며, **단수 취급**을 한다. a나 -s 대신 앞에 **a piece of/two pieces of**와 같은 **척도**^(=자)를 **붙여서 셈**을 한다.

Let me know **a piece of interview** information.
인터뷰 정보 하나만 알려주세요.

Internet **access** will help you study.
인터넷 접속을 해야 도움을 받을 수 있다.

The office needs **three pieces of furniture** now.
사무실은 지금 세 개의 가구가 필요하다.

We need the supervisors's **consent**.
우리는 지금 상사의 동의가 필요하다.

Put **a piece of luggage** here.

가방 하나를 여기에 올려놓으세요.

불가산 명사 예 : information(정보), access(접속), furniture(가구), consent(동의),
luggage(짐), advice(충고), equipment(장비), machinery(장비류),
stationary(문구류)

 실전문제

17 There's a displayer's position opening up which you'd be perfect
for, since you have dealt with a lot of _____.

(A) furniture   (B) furnitures
(C) a furniture   (D) the furnitures

18 Airline passengers are expected to pick up and recheck all of
their _____ before boarding their connecting flight.

(A) luggages   (B) luggage
(C) baggages   (D) package

19 We collect _____ about customer responses to put
ourselves in the customers' shoes in terms of how they are spending.

(A) informations   (B) the informations
(C) an information   (D) information

20 We found _____ to support the fact that our president
appropriated money for entertainment expenses.

(A) evidence   (B) evidences
(C) an evidence   (D) the evidence

3 사람 명사와 사물 명사

employee(고용주)-employment(고용-)   consultant(상담사)-consultation(상담)
supervisor(상사)-supervision(감독)   applicant(지원자)-application(지원서)
assistant(조수)-assistance(도움)   investor(투자자)-investment(투자)
instructor(강사)-instruction(교육)   participant(참석자)-participation(참석)

New **investors** will visit the shop in a minutes.
새 투자자들이 곧 가게를 방문할 겁니다.

Let's talk about our **investment** to your company.
당신 회사에 대한 우리의 투자에 대해서 이야기 해 봅시다.

Every job **applicant** should submit his resume.
모든 구직자들은 자기 이력서를 제출해야만 합니다.

Send us your **application** as soon as possible.
지원서를 가능한 빨라 우리에게 보내주세요.

The **employee** gets generous salary.
그 직원은 후한 월급을 받고 있다.

The president gave me the **employment**.
저 사장님이 내게 일자리를 주셨다.

 실전문제

21 A new _____ who is going to purchase the land for one million dollars will visit the real estate agency.

(A) consultant   (B) investor   (C) applicant   (D) assistant

22 Every job _____ should submit his resume and letter of self-introduction by e-mail by December 31th.

(A) employee   (B) participant   (C) supervisor   (D) applicant

23 To learn about possible retirement plans, please visit Real Estate Consulting for free _____ and financial support.

(A) investor   (B) investment   (C) consultant   (D) consultation

24 You can't get your money back for that sweater unless you have a _____ for it.

(A) receipt   (B) reception   (C) receiver   (D) recipe

4 채용 어휘 연구

1) **apply** v. 지원하다; n. **application** 지원, 지원서
   ex: 회사에 지원하다.

2) **submit** v. 제출하다; s. hand in
   ex: 이력서를 제출하다.

3) **candidate** n. 지원자; s. applicant
   ex: 지원자가 많다.

4) **eligible** a. 자격이 있는; n. **eligibility** 적임, 적격
   ex: 합격 될 자격이 있다.

5) **benefits** n. 복지 혜택, 수당; v. **benefit** 이익을 주다
   ex: 복지수당이 많다.

6) **compensation** n. 보상; v. **compensate** 보상하다

    ex: 금전적 보상을 원하다.

실전문제

25 Any employees who want to transfer to a local branch should
_____ an application to the personnel department.

(A) send   (B) submit   (C) give   (D) provide

26 Employees who had at least five years of experience of managerial
position are _____ for the sales manager position.

(A) enlisted   (B) suitable   (C) eligible   (D) good

5 독해 연구

New Exercise Kit

PortaGym turns ordinary stretching into serious exercise and gives you a complete workout at home or on the road. The gym can tone and shape all the muscle groups in your body. So unique and comprehensive is the gym that Olympic, college, and professional athletes use it as an integral part of their fitness program.

The compact design zips into a 16-inch case and tucks into your briefcase or carry-on. The PortaGym comes with a 27-inch lifting bar, jogging belt, 6-foot cable, door attachment, carrying case, an illustrated exercise booklet, and exercise video. $39.95

실전문제

27 What is being offered?

(A) Membership to a health club
(B) Gymnastic equipment
(C) Weights and Barbells
(D) An exercise set

28 Who is the intended audience for this advertisement?

(A) Business executives
(B) Olympic and professional athletes
(C) Fitness instructors
(D) Health professionals

29 Which claim is NOT made for this product?

(A) It is portable.
(B) It tones and shapes muscles.
(C) It helps you lose weight.
(D) It gives you a total workout.

30 What is the meaning of the word 'compact'?

(A) solid   (B) thick
(C) dense   (D) concise

CHAPTER 05 형용사

명사를 형용하는 품사의 준말로 **명사 앞 또는 뒤**에 놓여 그 **명사**를 **수식**한다.

1 형용사가 하는 일

1) 뒤 명사 수식

문장의 필수요소는 아니며, **뒤 명사를 수식**한다.

We make **durable** goods.
우리는 내구성이 있는 제품을 만듭니다.

The manager purchased **effective** equipment by mistake.
팀장님은 실수로 결함 있는 제품을 구매하셨다.

The program had a **beneficial** impact on residents.
그 프로그램은 거주민들에게 유익한 영향을 미쳤다.

2) 앞 명사 수식

문장의 필수요소는 아니며, 대개 **불완전 명사** 뒤에서 **앞 명사를 수식**한다.

Our company tries to make something **durable**.
우리 회사는 내구성이 강한 것 좀 만들려고 노력하고 있다.

I didn't do anything **special** during my vacation.
나는 내 휴가 중에 특별한 일을 하지 않았다.

I have something **private** to discuss with your boss.
나는 당신 상사와 얘기 할 사적인 게 좀 있다.

실전문제

01 Our company owes the bank more than 1,600 _____ owing to the recent business depression.

(A) million won   (B) millions won

(C) million wons   (D) millions wons

02 Most vocational colleges require all their students to gain _____ experience by working on the fields.

(A) practice   (B) practical   (C) practiced   (D) practicer

03 The family doctor said that my next routine dental appointment would be on Friday, _____ day of October, 2015.

(A) the fifth   (B) fifth   (C) five   (D) the five

04 When I was fired, I was nearly stone-broke; I had to keep body and soul together somehow with the greatest difficulty _____.

(A) imagine   (B) imaginable   (C) imaginably   (D) imagination

3) 주격 보어로 쓰임

문장의 필수 요소로, **2형식동사**의 **주격 보어**로 쓰인다.

Cooperation is **vital** for the success of any team project.
어떤 팀 프로젝트에서도 협동이 성공에 필수적이다.

His comment didn't seem **relevant** to the discussion.
그의 부언은 토론과 관련이 있어 보이지 않는다.

The goods are **defective** so should be recalled.
그 제품들은 결함이 있어 곧 회수되어야 한다.

4) 목적격 보어로 쓰임

문장의 필수 요소로, **5형식동사**의 **목적격 보어**로 쓰인다.

Our company considers the consumer service **vital**.
우리 회사는 고객서비스가 필수적이라고 여긴다.

The bad economy made investors **cautious**.
안 좋은 경제는 투자자들로 하여금 조심하게 만들었다.

I find the manager's words **worthless**.
나는 아직도 팀장님의 말씀이 일리 없다 고 생각한다.

 ## 실전문제

05 As a result of the serious electric power shortage, the government let people be _____ to electricity.

(A) economical   (B) economic   (C) economy   (D) economically

06 You will find the tallest building situated in the area which was _____ to the International Airport.

(A) closeness   (B) close   (C) closed   (D) closely

07 Due to bad sales over the last three years, ABC Industries has decided to make 3,000 employees _____.

(A) dismiss   (B) dismissing   (C) dismissed   (D) dismissal

08 That new animated movie Doctor Spider is _____ for children over the age of six, but probably too frightening for younger children.

(A) suit   (B) suiting   (C) suitable   (D) suits

2 형용사의 보충어

아래 happy 문장 (1)은 happy 만으로 의미 전달이 충분하나, (2)의 able 문장은 able 만으로 **의미 전달**이 **불충분**하다.

(1) I am **happy**.
(2) ※I am **able**.
(3) I am **able** to buy a BMW.

이럴 때 (3)처럼 able이 취하는 **to buy a car**를 able의 **보충어**라 부른다.

1) 전치사구를 보충어로 취하는 형용사

He is **good** at gambling.
그는 도박에 능하다.

The employee is **anxious** about the company's future.
그 직원은 회사의 미래에 대해 걱정을 한다.

The driver is **afraid** of driving at night.
기사는 야간에 운전하기를 두려워한다.

The factory worker is **familiar** with his district.
그 공장노동자는 그의 지역에 대해 익숙하다.

The manager was **sorry** for being late for the meeting.
팀장은 모임에 늦은 것에 미안해 했다.

This cell phone is too **similar** to that one.
이 핸드폰은 저 것과 똑 닮았다.

We are **dependent** on our team manager on that.

우리는 그 것에 관해서는 팀장에 의존한다.

2) That 절을 보충어로 취하는 형용사

I'm **sure** that the manager is honest.

팀장님이 정직하다는 것은 확실하다.

I'm **afraid** that I shall fail again.

다시 실패 할까 봐 두렵다.

3) To 부정사를 보충어로 취하는 형용사

I am **anxious** to submit my resume.

이력서 넣기를 갈망한다.

I am **afraid** to fail the company entrance exam.

입사시험 떨어질까 봐 걱정이다.

4) 명사를 보충어로 취하는 형용사

This product is **worth** 10,000 won.

이 상품은 만원의 가치가 있다.

We were really **busy** working on the other project.

우리는 다른 프로젝트를 하느라고 바빴어.

 실전문제

09 When ordered to visit the branch office, we delayed the departure until morning, because we were afraid _____ at night.

(A) at driving   (B) to drive

(C) drive   (D) driving

10 Even though the desktop computer is very _____ mine, my computer is more sophisticated and has 16 megabytes of RAM.

(A) similar to   (B) similar with

(C) familiar to   (D) familiar with

11 It's still not _____ that the shareholders' meeting will go ahead, since the board of directors turned down the proposal.

(A) sure   (B) definitive   (C) certain   (D) anxious

12 The bank, worth _____ this time last year, is now valued in the market at 20 billion dollars.

(A) of $ 200 billion   (B) $ 200 billion

(C) on $ 200 billion   (D) with $ 200 billion

❸ 업무 어휘 연구

1) **conduct** v. 수행하다; n. 수행; s. carry out

    ex: 설문조사를 실시하다.

2) **priority** n. 우선(권), a prior 우선의, 사전의

    ex: 이 일에 우선순위를 두다.

3) **negotiate** v. 협상하다; n. **negotiation** 협상

    ex: 임금 협상을 하다.

4) **acquisition** n. (기업) 인수; v. **acquire** 인수하다, 취득하다

    ex: 경쟁 회사를 인수하다.

5) **perform** n. 성과를 내다, 공연하다; n. **performance** 성과, 수행, 공연

   ex: 수행 평가를 하다.

6) **commitment** n. 헌신, 약속; v. **commit** 헌신하다, 약속하다

   ex: 회사에 헌신하다.

실전문제

13 Our company _____ background checks on potential employees living in local areas using video conference equipment.

   (A) conducts (B) negotiates (C) implements (D) acquires

14 The human resources department will _____ new contracts with recruits employed through the last company entrance exams.

   (A) commit (B) achieve (C) perform (D) negotiate

4 독해 연구

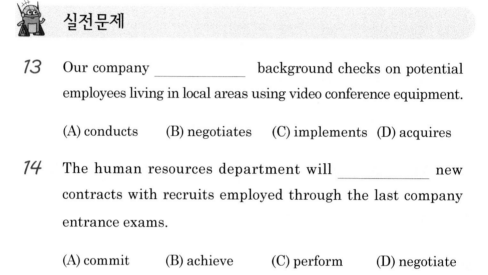

Attention Passengers

Only one percent of all luggage is lost, but if the initial on-the spot search by the airline representative fails, the traveler should write down a description of the luggage and hand it in to the Customer Relations Office before leaving the airport.

If the luggage is still missing after several days, the traveler should file a claim form. Airlines are liable for damages up to $750. For luggage worth more than $750, "excess valuation protection" is available at rates of 10 ¢ per $100 of coverage. Maximum coverage is $25,000, and some policies exclude particularly valuable or breakable items.

 실전문제

15 When should travelers file a claim form?

(A) Before leaving the airport
(B) Six or seven days after trip
(C) When contacted by the airline's office
(D) When submitting receipts

16 What is the standard limit that airlines must reimburse for lost luggage?

(A) 10 ¢   (B) $100   (C) $750   (D) $25,000

17 When might travelers NOT be able to buy "excess valuation protection" for their luggage?

(A) When only one percent of the contents has been damaged
(B) When their initials are missing from the suitcase
(C) When they have other insurance coverage
(D) When the contents are very fragile.

18 What is the meaning of the word 'spot'?

(A) site   (B) point   (C) location   (D) trouble

CHAPTER 06

동사
(조동사 · 시제 · 상)

1 조동사

동사 앞에서 동사를 도와 그 동사가 **의문, 완료, 진행, 허가, 가능, 의무, 필연** 등을 나타낼 수 있도록 **동사를 돕는 동사**를 **조동사**라 한다.

1) 주조동사

(1) Do

의문문이나 부정문을 만드는데 쓴다.

Do you submit your application?
지원서는 제출하셨지요?

I **didn't** submit my application yet.
지원서 아직 제출하지 못 했습니다.

(2) Have

완료문을 만드는데 쓴다.

I **have** read my application several times.
제 지원서를 여러 차례 읽어보았습니다.

(3) Be

진행문이나 **수동문**을 만드는데 쓴다.

The supervisor **is** reading my resume.^(진행문)
관리자께서 내 이력서를 읽고 있는 중입니다.

The resume **is** read by the manager.^(수동문)
팀장님이 이력서를 읽었다.

2) 서법조동사

동사에다 **허가, 가능, 능력, 의지, 예측, 의무, 필연** 등을 부가 하고자 할 때 동사 앞에 붙이는 조동사를 말한다.

(1) May

허가와 약한 추측을 나타낸다.

You **may** smoke here.^(허가)
여기서 담배 피워도 좋다.

The cause of his death **may** be his heavy smoking.^(약한 추측)
그의 사망 원인이 아마 그의 심한 흡연인 것 같다.

(2) Can

허가, 약한 추측, 능력을 나타낸다.

You **can** smoke here.^(허가)
여기서 담배 피워도 좋다.

Smoking **can** cause cancer.^(약한 추측)
흡연이 암을 유발 할 수 있다.

The team leader **can** solve the problem by himself. (=is able to)^(능력)
팀장님 혼자서 그 문제를 해결할 수 있다.

(3) Will

예측과 의지를 나타낸다.

I **will** be 21 tomorrow.^(추측)
내년에 21살이 된다.

I **will** not speak to him.(의지)
그에게 말을 걸지 않을 것이다.

(4) Shall

화자의 **의지**나, **상대**의 **의지**를 나타낸다.

You **shall** have the money.(화자의 의지)
그 돈 가져가게 되고 말거다.

Shall I open the door?(상대의 의지)
문 열어도 될 가요?

 실전문제

01 The company _____ moved to its new building since
    it is now suffering from severe financial difficulties.

    (A) may have   (B) may not have
    (C) not may have   (D) may well

02 Because he had directly involved in the project, he _____
    answer questions from the press effortlessly.

    (A) can   (B) could   (C) must   (D) should

03 When the president said "I really feel drowsy." the secretary
    responded with " _____ get you some coffee?"

    (A) Shall I   (B) Can I   (C) Will I   (D) Should I

04 The invitation stated that the reception for the company's
    10th anniversary _____ begin at 7 o'clock p.m.

    (A) will   (B) can   (C) would   (D) should

(5) Must

강한 의무와 **확실한 추측**을 나타낸다.

You **must** work overtime.^(강한 의무)
야근 해야만 합니다.

The man over there **must** be my friend.^(확실한 추측)
저기 저 사람 내 친구 임에 100% 틀림없다.

(6) Should

약한 의무와 **약한 추측**을 나타낸다.

You **should** work overtime.^(약한 의무)
야근 해 주십시오.

The man over there **should** be my friend.^(약한 추측)
저기 저 사람 내 친구인 것 같다.

 실전문제

05 The assistant manager _____ have missed the shuttle bus or he would surely be the office by now.

   (A) could   (B) must   (C) would   (D) should

06 You should take care lest you _____ make the same mistake which you made after you had entered the company.

   (A) might   (B) must   (C) would   (D) should

07 I do not know where the marketing director is, but considering that his phone is here he _____ out for a while.

   (A) must have gone   (B) should have gone
   (C) would have gone   (D) went

08 To become a member of civic association, you _____ attend three times a month and pay your fee regularly.

(A) might   (B) should   (C) would   (D) could

2 시제

동사의 어형 변화(play-played-played, playing)를 통해 **문장**의 **시간 관계를 표현한 것**을 **시제**라 하고, **현재, 과거, 미래의 3시제**가 있다.

1) 현재 시제

현재 일어나는 **일**을 동사에 **−s를 붙여 표기**한다. 부사 now, always, usually, generally, currently, often, regularly, every− 등과 함께 쓰인다.

(1) 현재의 동작이나 상태

He **oversees** the sales department.
그가 판매과를 관장한다.

Employees **are** hungry now.
직원들은 지금 배가 고프다.

(2) 일반적인 사실

The earth **goes** around the sun.
지구는 태양의 두레를 돈다.

Two plus two **is** four.
둘 더하기 둘은 넷이다.

(3) 현재 습관

The shuttle bus **departs** from the airport every hour.
셔틀버스는 매시에 공항을 출발한다.

My colleague always **opens** office door.
내 동료는 항상 사무실 문을 연다.

실전문제

09 A company's purchasing departments are responsible for supplying the goods that each office _____ for its operation.

(A) require   (B) required
(C) will require   (D) requires

10 Sales staff always work in the office in the morning, and they _____ their customers in the afternoon.

(A) visit   (B) visited
(C) will visit   (D) have visited

2) 과거 시제

과거에 일어난 **일**을 동사에 **-ed를 붙여 표기**한다. 부사 yesterday, go, before, previously, once, recently, last- 등과 함께 쓰인다.

(1) 과거의 동작이나 상태

I **had** a late dinner yesterday.
나 어제 늦은 저녁을 먹었다.

I **was** happy last night.
나 어제 밤 행복했었다.

(2) 과거 습관

I recently **went** to bed at 12.
나는 최근에 12시에 잤다.

Previously, only those aged over 70 **were** entitled.
이전에는 70세 이상의 노인들만 자격이 되었다.

실전문제

11 The new employees had gone over the newly amended employment contract before they _____.

(A) signed it　　(B) will sign it　　(C) sign it　　(D) had signed it

12 Several members of the audience _____ and demanded their money back since the play was boring.

(A) walk out　　　　　　　　(B) walked out
(C) had walked out　　　　　(D) walked

13 Scarcely had the employee locked the office door of his office when the door key _____ with a snap.

(A) breaks　　　　　　　　(B) was breaking
(C) broke　　　　　　　　(D) had broken

14 Two female CEOs have served in our company since the first woman president _____ five years ago.

(A) elected　　(B) had elected　　(C) was elected　　(D) have elected

3) 미래 시제

미래에 일어날 **일**에 대한 **예측**이나 **의지**를 will, be going to, be to로 표기한다. 부사 tomorrow, soon, shortly, next- 등과 함께 쓰인다.

(1) 미래에 대한 예측

I will be 21 tomorrow.
나 내일 21살 된다.

We are to launch a new item tomorrow.
우리 회사 낼일 새 제품을 출시 할 예정이다.

(2) 미래에 대한 의지

I am going to become a casino dealer after graduation.
나 졸업하고 카지노 딜러가 될 거다.

 실전문제

15 Several prominent figures who are involved in the scandal
_____ before the investigating committee.

(A) will appear   (B) will be appear
(C) are to appear   (D) is to appear

16 Our company enforced new price policy recently and the new
prices _____ into effect on January 2.

(A) will go   (B) would go   (C) went   (D) had gone

4) 미래 시제의 예외

시간 부사절(when, as, once, while, after, before, as soon as, until 절)이나 **조건 부사절**(if 절)**의 시제**가 **미래일 때**, 영어에서는 will을 생략하고 **현재 시제를 사용**해야만 한다.

When I **graduate**, I'll be 21.
네가 졸업할 때는 21살이 될 거다.

If you **get** HSK 5, you'll be accepted by the Paradise Casino.
HSK 5급을 따면, 파라다이스 카지노에 합격될 것이다.

 ## 실전문제

17 When the shipment which our counter company has sent _____ in, I will dispatch it to the proper departments.

(A) will come　　(B) comes　　(C) will come　　(D) comes

18 The stock market will flourish if the news that Korea will be reunified in the near future _____ around the Wall Street.

(A) gets out　　(B) got out　　(C) will get out　　(D) would get out

3 상

상이란 **동사**의 **동작**이나 **상태**가 **표현**되어 나타나는 **방식**으로, 영어에는 종료^{(=다}했다⁾를 나타내는 **완료상**과, 진행^(=하는 중이다)을 나타내는 **진행상**, 두 가지가 있다.

1) 완료상

한국어의 '**~을 다 했다**'를 영어에서는 '**have+p.p.**'로 나타낸다.

(1) 현재 완료

과거에 발생하여 **현재에 와서 완성된 것**을 have+p.p.로 나타내며, 완료, 경험, 계속, 결과로 해석한다. **for**–^(-동안), **since**–^(-동안), **over**–^(-동안), **already**^(벌써), **before**^(전에) 등과 함께 쓰인다.

The sales manage **has** already **completed** his sales quota.
영업부장님께서는 벌써 자기 판매 할당량을 채우셨다.(완료)

I **have** never **seen** such a person before.
난 그 사람을 전에 본 적이 없다.(경험)

(2) 과거 완료

과거 이전에 발생하여 **과거에 와서 완성된 것**을 had+p.p.로 나타내며, 완료, 경험, 계속, 결과로 해석한다. before−^(−전에)와 함께 쓰인다.

The retailer **had inquire**d about the prices before he placed an order.
그 소매상은 주문내기 전에 가격에 대해 문의를 했다.(완료)

I **had** never **seen** such a person before.
난 전에 그런 사람을 본 적이 없었다.(경험)

(3) 미래 완료

과거나 현재에 발생하여 **미래에 와서 완성된 것**을 will have+p.p.로 나타내며, 완료로 해석한다. **by/till+미래 시각**^(−까지)와 함께 쓰인다.

By tomorrow we**'ll have paid** the buildings utility bill.
내일까지는 건물 공공요금은 지불이 완료 될 것이다.

I **will have worked** here for 30 years till the end of the year.
이 달 말이면 내가 여기서 30년을 일 하게 된다.

 실전문제

19 By 2022, they _____ at least 40 million barrels of oil a day if the West is to avoid the crippling energy crisis.

(A) will have produced   (B) produce
(C) will produce   (D) produced

20 The government has been anxious to modernize the infrastructures
in the regions which _____ behind in the last decade.

(A) fell   (B) had fallen   (C) falls   (D) has fallen

21 The night duty employee, woke up at the sound of the
explosion and inquired what _____ the safety guard.

(A) had happened of   (B) happens from
(C) happened from   (D) has happened of

22 By the time he retires next month because of the age limit of
60, he _____ the company for 30 years.

(A) has served   (B) will have served
(C) serves   (D) served

2) 진행상

우리말의 '~하는 중이다'를 영어에서는 'be+-ing'로 나타낸다.

(1) 현재 진행

현재에 **진행** 중인 **일**을 be+-ing로 나타내며, '현재 -이 진행 중이다'로 해석
한다.

My manager **is meeting** with a client now at 10.
지금 10시 우리 팀장님은 고객을 만나고 계신다.

(2) 과거 진행

과거에 **진행** 중이었던 **일**을 was+-ing로 나타내며, '과거에 -이 진행 중 이었
다'로 해석한다.

My manager **was meeting** with a client yesterday at 10.
어제 10시 우리 팀장님은 고객을 만나고 계셨었다.

(3) 미래 진행

미래에 **진행** 중 **일**을 **will be+-ing**로 나타내며, '미래에 -이 진행 중일 것이다'로 해석한다.

My manager **will be meeting** with a client tomorrow at 10.
내일 10시 우리 팀장님은 고객을 만나고 계실 것이다.

 실전문제

23 When we arrived at the company party, the party had already begun and all the employees _____ drinks.

    (A) were having   (B) had

    (C) has   (D) are having

24 When the delegation arrived in Mexico, it _____ for four days, so the roads were very muddy.

    (A) was raining   (B) has rained

    (C) would be raining   (D) had been raining

4 조직 어휘 연구

1) **board** n. 판, 회의탁자, 이사회; v. 탑승하다
    ex: 이사회에 참석하다.

2) **administrative** a. 관리의, 행정의; v. **administrate** 관리하다, 운영하다
    ex: 회사를 운영하다.

3) **promotion** n. 승진, 홍보, 판촉; v. **promote** 승진시키다, 판촉하다

　　ex: 팀장으로 승진하다.

4) **transfer** v. 전근가다, 전학가다, 넘기다; s. relocate

　　ex: 지방으로 전근가다.

5) **managerial** a. 관리⁽상⁾의; v. **manage** 경영하다, 관리하다

　　ex: 매니저 자리로 승진하다.

6) **oversee** v. 감독하다; s. supervise

　　ex: 근로자들을 감독하다.

실전문제

25 One of my colleague submitted a request to _____ to an overseas branch office to send his kids to the universities there.

(A) transfer　　　　　(B) commute

(C) transact　　　　　(D) escape

26 The new president and his cabinet will continue the efforts to simplify _____ processes of the government.

(A) adventurous　　　(B) administrative

(C) admiring　　　　(D) adjoining

5 독해 연구

Atherosclerosis

The No. 1 killer of Americans is heart disease. Each year over one million persons suffer from heart attacks and of this number over 700,000 die. In fact one out of every five men in America will die from coronary heart disease before they reach sixty years of age.

One of the main causes of heart disease is a lack of good eating habits. Atherosclerosis, the clogging and narrowing of the blood vessels, with fat, is increased 3 to 6 times when you eat too much cholesterol and 8 times when you have high blood pressure. Smoking is also a factor which increase coronary heart disease three to six times.

If you are 10 percent overweight, the risk is increased 10 to 13 percent. Lack of exercise is also another risk factor. There is no single cause of atherosclerosis, but how you eat is extremely important.

 실전문제

27 Eating too much cholesterol, according to this article?

    (A) is the main cause of atherosclerosis.

    (B) will restrict the flow of blood in the blood vessels.

    (C) increases the risk of death by at least 10 percent.

    (D) makes you want to smoke more.

28 Heart disease kill?

    (A) more people in the world than any other disease.

    (B) over one million people in America each year.

    (C) 20 percent of the men in America under 60.

    (D) over 700,000 men in America each year.

29 To reduce the risk of atherosclerosis you should?

    (A) stop smoking.

    (B) watch your diet.

    (C) have your blood vessels widened.

    (D) reduce your weight by 10%.

30 What is the meaning of the word 'clogging'?

    (A) hindering   (B) congesting

    (C) blocking   (D) passing

부사

동사의 **동작**이나 **상태**가 **언제, 어디서, 어떻게** 발생했는가를 나타내 주는 **동사 수식어**(adverb)를 **부사**라고 한다.

1 부사의 기능

1) 동사를 수식한다.

The marketing manager deals with matters **prudently**.
영업부장님은 일들을 신중하게 처리하신다.

The shop manager closed the door **early**.
상점 주인은 점포 문을 일찍 닫았다.

2) 형용사를 수식한다.

The sales manager is **highly** intelligent.
판매부장님은 대단히 재능이 좋으시다.

3) 부사를 수식한다.

The accounting manager knows accounting **very** well.
경리부장님은 회계를 매우 잘 아신다.

2 부사의 형태

부사는 대개 **형용사**에 **−ly**를 붙여 쓰거나, **형용사 그대로** 쓰거나, **혼합**해서 쓴다.

1) 형용사 +ly 형

You can get to the building **easily**.
그 빌딩에 쉽게 갈 수 있다.

Our company didn't developed any goods yet **lately**.
최근 우리 회사는 아직 신제품을 개발하지 못했다.

2) 형용사=부사 형

My watch is 5 minutes **fast**.^(형용사)
내 시계는 5분 빠르다.

→ The marketing manager speaks **fast**.^(부사)
영업부장님은 말씀을 빠르게 하신다.

I got a **collect** call yesterday.^(형용사)
어제 수신자 부담 전화 한통 받았다.

→ I want everyone to call me **collect**.^(부사)
나는 누구든 내게 수신자 부담으로 전화하길 원한다.

3) 혼합형

위 두 가지 형이 함께 쓰인다.

I was **wrongly** informed.^(부사)
나는 그릇되게 전달 받았다.

→ He guessed **wrong**.^(부사)
그는 추측을 잘못했다.

We won the success **cheaply**.^(부사)
우리는 쉽게 성공을 거뒀다.

→ She got the item **cheap**.^(부사)
그녀는 그 제품을 싸게 샀다.

실전문제

01 The business success in the _____ competitive global market depends on the ability for the management to lower costs.

(A) bitter   (B) bitterly   (C) right   (D) rightly

02 The best book on physical fitness will enable you to find out what your condition is _____ now.

(A) righteous   (B) rightly   (C) right   (D) rightfully

03 This booklet explains diamond cutting process which is an _____ complicated and precise one.

(A) extreme   (B) extremely   (C) extreme   (D) extremely

04 The office building was slightly damaged by the earthquake, but the building inspector said that it was still _____ sound.

(A) structure   (B) structura   (C) structurally   (D) structuring

③ 부사의 종류

1) 장소 · 방법 · 시간 부사

문장 끝에 **장소, 방법, 시간** 순서로 온다.

(1) 장소 부사

I ate lunch **there**.
나는 거기서 점심을 먹었다.

(2) 방법 부사

The manager behaved **badly**.
팀장님은 나쁘게 처신하셨다.

(3) 시간 부사

I met her two years **ago**.^(과거)
그녀를 2년 전에 만났다.

I had built the house **a month before**.^(과거 완료)
그 집을 한 달 전에 지었다.

I haven't seen her **since** January.^(현재 완료)
1월 이후 그녀를 보질 못했다.

He has **already** read the resume.^(완료)
그는 벌써 이력서를 읽었다.

I have not finished the application **yet**.^(미완료)
아직 지원서를 작성하지 못했다.

2) 빈도 · 부정 부사

빈도나 **부정**을 나타내며 그 정도는 다음과 같다.

always(100%)-frequently(80%)-usually(70%)-often(60%)-sometimes(50%)-occasionally(40%)-seldom(30%)-rarely(20%)-hardly(10%)-never(0%)

The boss **sometimes** sends me an email.
상사는 가끔씩 내게 이메일을 보내신다.

The director **seldom** goes to work by car.
이사님은 결코 차로 출근하지 않으신다.

3) 초점 · 정도 · 동사 강조 부사

찍어서 말하거나, 그 **정도**를 말하거나, 동사를 **직접 강조** 할 때 쓴다.

(1) 초점 부사

Only the team manager called me today.
오늘은 팀장님만이 내게 전화하셨다.

(2) 정도 부사

The president loves the employees **very** much.(원급 수식)
회장님은 직원들을 대단히 많이 사랑하신다.

The launch was **much** worse than I thought.(비교급 수식)
출시는 생각보다 훨씬 안 좋았다.

(3) 동사 강조 부사

The employees **gladly** accepted the president's invitation.
직원들은 기꺼이 회장님의 초청을 받아들였다.

실전문제

05 Although the mechanic gains _____ amount he can support his family thanks to the free company apartment.

(A) only smal (B) small only
(C) enough small (D) small enough

06 The investigation committee has not decided how it can cope with the manager's misappropriation of company goods _____.

(A) already (B) yet
(C) anymore (D) still

07   Since the employee worked overtime and he could not get up early today, he arrived at the meeting _____.

    (A) late too much   (B) much late too
    (C) much too late   (D) late much too

08   The president of the corporation has _____ arrived in Copenhagen and will meet with the Minister of Trade on Monday morning.

    (A) still   (B) yet   (C) already   (D) soon

4 개발 어휘 연구

1) **develop** v. 개발하다; n. **development** 개발, 발전
   ex: 신제품을 개발하다.

2) **demonstrate** v. 시연하다; n. **demonstration** 시연, 설명, 시위
   ex: 새 기계를 시연하다.

3) **available** a. 이용 가능한; v. **avail** 쓸모가 있다
   ex: 언제 가능해요?

4) **research** n. 조사, 연구; v. 조사하다, 연구하다
   ex: 조사와 연구를 시행하다.

5) **investigate** v. 조사하다; n. **investigation** 조사
   ex: 경리부장의 비리를 조사하다.

6) **monitor** v. (추적) 관찰하다; n. 화면, 모니터, 감시 장치
   ex: 주가 변동을 관찰해보세요.

실전문제

09 That entire training programs we are currently providing with foreign clients are _____ to your company.

(A) available   (B) fruitful   (C) acceptable   (D) believable

10 The market research team is going to _____ various reasons why the product does not appeal to local customers.

(A) prevent   (B) demonstrate (C) investigate (D) develop

5 독해 연구

Workshops

Author: Dinesh Joshi
Date: 9/22 3 PM
To: All Department-Level Managers
Subject: Meetings and Reports

Message Contents

Our annual management training workshops will be held in June. One series of 3-day seminars is scheduled for June 7 to 9. Another series is scheduled for June 14 to 16. Please select the series that is most convenient for you and be prepared to sign up at our monthly status meeting next Wednesday. Also, consider this a reminder to prepare your sales reports for the meeting and the survey form you received last week.

실전문제

11 What is the purpose of this e-mail message?

(A) To provide the outline for the management workshops
(B) To take a survey of all department level managers
(C) To provide the managers with an updated schedule
(D) To prepare the managers for their Wednesday meeting

12 How many times a year are the management training workshops held?

(A) Once a year   (B) Twice a year
(C) Three times a year   (D) Monthly

13 Before the meeting, the managers must do all of the following EXCEPT

(A) sign up for the training workshops
(B) prepare their sales reports.
(C) decide which series of seminars they want to take.
(D) complete their survey forms.

14 What is the meaning of the word 'reminder'?

(A) memorial   (B) informer
(C) demander   (D) advisor

CHAPTER
08

대명사

'나는 **철수**를 안다. **철수**는 잘 생겼다.' 라고 같은 명사 '**철수**'를 반복해서 쓰지 않고 '나는 **철수**를 안다. 그는 잘 생겼다.' 라고 명사 '**철수**'를 '**그**'로 바꿔서 사용하는 것을 **대명사**라 한다.

1 인칭대명사

주로 **사람**을 지칭하는 **대명사**를 **인칭대명사**라 한다. 인칭대명사는 문장 안에서 어떤 역할을 하느냐에 따라 **주격, 소유격, 목적격**으로 나누어진다.

1인칭 : I-my-me, we-our-us
2인칭 : you-your-you, you-your-you
3인칭 : he-his-him, she-her-her, it-its-it, they-their-them

1) 주격

I wants a full refund.
저는 전액 환불을 원합니다.

2) 소유격

My friend wants an exchange for a new one.
친구는 새 것으로의 교환을 원합니다.

3) 목적격

The clerk gave **her** a new one.
점원은 새 것 하나를 그녀에게 가져다주었다.

실전문제

01 It was not _____ but the travel agency who cancelled the trip because tourists don't travel in bad weather.

(A) I (B) my (C) me (D) mine

02 The judging committee of the best salesperson contest decided to award the first prize to the new employee and _____.

(A) myself (B) I (C) my (D) me

03 Nowadays the Internet have made _____ easier to store and exchange data conveniently and accurately.

(A) one (B) its (C) ones (D) it

04 Anybody who will not try to help the other employees develop _____ abilities does not deserve to have colleagues.

(A) their (B) his (C) its (D) her

2 소유대명사

mine(나의 것), yours(너의 것) 과 같이 **소유자의 것**을 나타내는 **대명사**를 소유대명사라 한다. 소유대명사는 **주어, 목적어, 보어**로 쓰인다.

1인칭 : me 2인칭 : yours 3인칭 : his, hers, theirs

1) 주어로 사용

Let's use my computer because **yours** is too slow.
당신께 너무 느리니 내 컴퓨터를 쓰지요.

2) 목적어로 사용

He lost his computer, so he is using **mine**.
그 사람 자기 컴퓨터 고장 나서 내꺼 쓰고 있다.

3) 보어로 사용

This user manual is mine and that is **yours**.
이 사용자 매뉴얼은 내 꺼 고 저게 당신 꺼다.

실전문제

05 It looks as though your flight seat number will be near
_____ for our flight to Amsterdam.

    (A) mine   (B) me   (C) I   (D) my

06 After he became the vice president, he realized that it was
the company's welfare that mattered, not _____.

    (A) theirs   (B) his   (C) them   (D) he

07 The employee passed through New York on his way to Boston
branch office and there he stopped overnight at his _____.

    (A) sister's   (B) sister   (C) sisters'   (D) sister

08 Most of the self-introductions contained only text, but
_____ included some photos and graphs.

    (A) I   (B) my   (C) myself   (D) mine

3 재귀대명사

myself^(나 자신), **yourself**^(너 자신)처럼 '**-자신**'을 의미하는 말을 **재귀대명사**라 한다.

1인칭 : myself-ourselves
2인칭 : yourself-yourselves
3인칭 : himself-herself-itself-themselves

1) 동사나 전치사의 **목적어가 주어와 같은 사람을 지칭할 때 재귀대명사**를 사용한다.

The guest introduced **himself**.
손님은 자신을 소개했다.

The worker looked at **himself** in the mirror.
그 노동자는 거울로 자신을 보았다.

2) 의미를 강조할 때 쓰인다.

The manager did it **himself**.
팀장님은 자신이 그것을 하셨다.

3) 숙어로 쓴다.

She decorated the whole wall **by herself**.^(=alone, 혼자서, 혼자 힘으로)
그녀는 벽 전체를 혼자 힘으로 장식했다.

 실전문제

09 When my airplane took off for Amsterdam, I felt _____
    very happy because I was finally going to Europe.

    (A) myself   (B) my   (C) mime   (D) me

10   The delegation bought some leather coats for the executives and some imitation leather coats for _____ .

(A) them   (B) themselves   (C) theirs   (D) they

11   The manager said from the chef's point of view, the presentation of the food is as important as the food's taste _____ .

(A) of it   (B) of itself   (C) itself   (D) in itself

12   Because his partner had to go to Sydney, Mr. Zazueta had to finish work on the advertising campaign by _____ .

(A) his own   (B) himself   (C) alone   (D) solo

4 지시대명사

명사를 지시 할 때 쓰는 **대명사를 지시대명사**라 한다.

1) **가까운 것**을 지칭 할 때는 **this**를, **먼 것**을 지칭 할 때는 **that**을 쓴다.

This smart phone is mine and **that** is yours.
이 핸드폰은 내 것이고 저 핸드폰은 네 것이다.

2) **앞 문장 전체**를 대신 할 때는 this나 that을 모두 쓴다.

My colleague drove me to the airport, and **this/that** helped me to board in time.
동료가 공항까지 태워다 두었고 그 것이 제 시간에 탑승하는데 도움을 주었다.

3) 앞에 나온 명사의 **반복을 피해 that**(those)를 쓴다.

The prices of commodities of Seoul is more expensive than **that** of Busan.
서울의 물가가 부산의 물가보다 더 비싸다.

4) **일반인**을 지칭 할 때는 **those**^(-하는 자들)를 쓴다.

The workshop is designed for **those** who don't know how to use the database.
그 워크숍은 데이터베이스를 어떻게 사용하는지 모르는 사람들을 위해 만들어졌다.

 실전문제

13 Among the customers only three percent of _____ who responded said the new item was useless.

(A) those   (B) that   (C) this   (D) these

14 Since the sales department worked very hard, the sales figures of the department surpassed _____ of other competitors.

(A) those   (B) that   (C) this   (D) these

5 부정대명사

정해지지 않은 대상을 가리킬 때에는 **부정대명사**를 사용한다.

1) 두 개일 때

하나에는 one을, **다른 하나**에는 the other를 쓴다.

There are two smart phones. **One** is mine and **the other** is yours.
두 개의 핸드폰이 있다, 하나는 내 것이고, 다른 하나는 네 것이다.

2) 세 개일 때

첫 번째 것에는 one을, **두 번째** 것에는 another를, **마지막** 것에는 the other를 쓴다.

There are three smart phones. **One** is A's, **another** is B's and **the other** is C's.
세 개의 핸드폰이 있다, 하나는 A의 것이고, 다른 하나는 B의 것이고, 마지막은 C의 것이다.

3) 세 개 이상일 때

첫 번째 것에는 one을, **두 번째** 것에는 another를, **나머지 중 일부**에는 others 를, **나머지 전부**에는 the others를 쓴다.

There are many smart phones. **One** is A's, **another** is B's, **others** are C's and **the others** are D's.
여러 개의 핸드폰이 있다, 하나는 A의 것이고, 다른 하나는 B의 것이고, 나머지 중 일부는 C의 것이고, 나머지 모두는 D의 것이다.

4) '서로'의미일 때

둘 사이 서로에는 each other를, **셋 이상**에서 **서로**에는 one another를 쓴다.

New employees should support **one another**.
신규 직원들은 서로 도와야 한다.

5) 긍정문에 some, 의문문에 any

May I have **some** coffee, please?^(긍정의 의미)
커피 좀 주시겠어요?

Hardly **any**body had the chance to go on a journey to the antarctic.^(부정의 의미)
누구도 남극으로 여행갈 기회도 거의 가보지 못했다.

6) 각각에 each, 모든에 every

Each of us has his own claims.^(대명사)
우리들은 각각 자기의 주장이 있다.

Every employee speaks well of the presidents.^(형용사)
모든 직원들은 회장님을 좋게 말을 한다.

7) 영(=0)에는 none, 대부분의에는 most

None of the employees is present.
직원 중 아무도 참석하지 않았다.

Most of the employees like bonus.
직원 모두는 보너스를 좋아한다.

 실전문제

15 As we are a multinational company, some of my colleagues are from America, others are from Europe, and _____ are from Asia.

    (A) rest   (B) the other   (C) the others   (D) others

16 According to the Government reports, _____ economists expect the economy will recover from the economic recession.

    (A) the most   (B) most of the   (C) most of   (D) the most of

17 Negotiable instruments such as personal checks may ordinarily be transferred to _____ by endorsement.

    (A) anothers   (B) others   (C) another   (D) other

18 The new president should be stopped _____ dozen yards by the employees who wanted to congratulate him.

    (A) each   (B) every   (C) all   (D) both

6 판매 어휘 연구

1) **reduction** n. 할인, 감소; v. **reduce** 줄이다, 낮추다
    ex: 속도를 줄이세요.

2) **installment** n. 할부, 분납; v. **install** 설치하다

    ex: 핸드폰을 할부로 구입했다.

3) **complaint** n. 불만 (사항); v. **complain** 불평하다, 항의하다

    ex: 몇 개의 불만이 들어왔다.

4) **inquiry** n. 문의; v. **inquire** 문의하다

    ex: 가격을 문의하다.

5) **guarantee** n. 보장; v. 보장하다; s. ensure

    ex: 이 상품의 품질을 보장하다.

6) **recall** n. 회수, 회상, 소환; v. 회수하다, 상기하다

    ex: 자동차 500대를 리콜하다.

 실전문제

19 Our customer service representatives are always busy dealing with customer _____ about products.

    (A) complaints   (B) recalls
    (C) replacements   (D) inquiries

20 The company _____ you that it delivers the items by noon on the next business day.

    (A) recalls   (B) guarantees
    (C) investigates   (D) expires

7 독해 연구

Course Registration

A $100 deposit per person is required for the 5-day course and $50 per person for the 2-day course. Deposits are refundable if notice of cancellation is received at least 14 days prior to reservation period, less a $10 handling charge. Deposit will not be refunded if cancellation is received less than 14 days prior to reservation period.

Deposit may be transferred to another session if notice of change is received at least 7 days prior to original date of enrollment. Transfer of deposit to another session is contingent upon availability of space in that session.

실전문제

21 Which of the following would be the best heading for this notice?

(A) Procedures for Depositing Checks
(B) Availability of Registration Forms
(C) Spring Course Offerings
(D) Policy on Withdrawals

22 How much most you pay if you cancel your registration three weeks before a session begins?

(A) Nothing   (B) $5   (C) $10   (D) $50

23   What determines if your deposit can be transferred to a different course?

(A) If you have paid the handling charge
(B) If there is any space left in the second course
(C) If the first course is canceled because of low enrollment
(D) If your original space can be filled

24   What is the meaning of the word 'deposit'?

(A) premium   (B) payment
(C) subscription   (D) installmen

CHAPTER 09

전치사

in, on, at 같은 전치사는 ^(전치사의 목적어인) **'명사 앞에 위치하는^(=전치) 품사'**의 준말로, 뒤에 오는 명사와 함께 **'전치사+명사' 구**를 이루어 앞의 **명사**나 **동사**를 **수식**하는 대표적인 기능어다.

1 전치사구가 하는 일

1) 형용사로 쓰임

(1) 명사를 수식한다.

We always use the conference room **at the back of the employee lounge**.
우리는 항상 직원 휴게실 뒤에 있는 회의실을 사용한다.

(2) 주격 보어로 쓰인다.

This manual is **about how customers use hotel facilities**.
이 매뉴얼은 고객들이 호텔 시설을 어떻게 이용하느냐에 관한 것이다.

2) 부사로 쓰임

(1) 동사를 수식한다.

The exact meeting hour of tomorrow will be decided **after the dinner meeting**.
정확한 내일 모임 시간은 저녁 모임 후에 결정될 것이다.

(2) 형용사를 수식한다.

The president was popular **during his service**.
회장님은 재직 중에 인기가 좋았다.

2 장소 전치사

1) 점 · 면 · 공간 전치사

	–로	–밖으로	–에	–밖에
점	to	away from	at	away from
면	on	off	on	off
공간	in	ut of	in	ut of

(1) I went **to** the office by car.
차로 사무실로 갔다.

(2) I went **away from** my house.
집 밖으로 나갔다.

(3) I am **at** my office now.
지금 사무실에 있다.

(4) I am **away from** my house now.
지금 집 밖에 있다.

(5) I got **on** the shuttle bus.
셔틀버스에 올라탔다.

(6) I got **off** the shuttle bus.
셔틀버스 밖으로 내렸다.

(7) I am **on** the shuttle bus now.
지금 셔틀버스에 있다.

(8) I am **off** the shuttle bus now.
지금 셔틀버스 밖에 있다.

(9) I came **in** the office.
사무실로 들어갔다.

(10) I went **out of** my house.
집 밖으로 나갔다.

(11) I am **in** the office now.
지금 사무실에 있다.

(12) I am **out of** my house now.
지금 집 밖에 있다.

 ## 실전문제

01 The factory which the has been built to distribute products to the downtown area is several miles _____ the main road.

(A) off   (B) on   (C) in   (D) at

02 The president's bonus provided the employees with a great opportunity to have a good impression _____ him.

(A) in   (B) on   (C) to   (D) by

03 He is very efficient and has an excellent background but does not like working _____ deadlines.

(A) to   (B) for   (C) at   (D) in

04 Sales rose _____ 6% in the second half of the year thanks to a major order that we received from the Netherlands.

(A) at   (B) by   (C) in   (D) of

2) 상·하·전·후 전치사

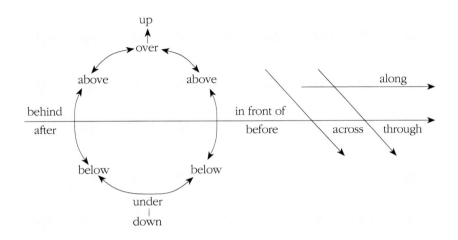

(1) Let's meet **on** Chongno Street.
종로 3가에서 만납시다.

(2) There is a fly **beneath** the table.
테이블 아래에 파리 한 마리가 앉아있다.

(3) There is a bridge **over** the river.
강 위에 다리가 하나 놓여 있다.

(4) A cat is lying **under** the table.
강아지 한 마리가 테이블 아래에 누워있다.

(5) He climbed **up** a tree.
그는 나무위로 올라갔다.

(6) We went **down** the stairs.
우리는 계단을 내려갔다.

(7) The mountain rises **above** the plain.
그 산은 평원위에 솟아 있다.

(8) The sun sank **below** the horizon.
해가 수평선 아래로 졌다.

(9) She stood just **in front of** the office building.
그녀는 사무실 빌딩 바로 앞에 서있다.

(10) The car is **behind** the bus.
차가 버스 앞에 놓여 있다.

(11) They are working **along** the river.
그들은 강을 따라 걷고 있다.

(12) He worked **across** the street.
그는 도로를 건너갔다.

(13) He swam **through** the pool water.
그는 풀장을 가로질러 수영을 했다.

 실전문제

05 Though most staff have worked overtime, the software project is weeks _____ schedule for unknown reasons.

(A) in   (B) on   (C) to   (D) behind

06 The committee walked _____ the quiet hallway to go to the president's office at the end of the floor.

(A) along   (B) in   (C) across   (D) on

07 The Brunswick Explorer is a submersible robotic vehicle designed to search for mineral deposits far _____ the surface of the sea.

(A) between   (B) below   (C) behind   (D) beyond

08 Complete the buildings on time and _____ budget so that we move there before January and without further funding.

(A) in   (B) on   (C) to   (D) behind

3) 부분·근접·사이·주위 전치사

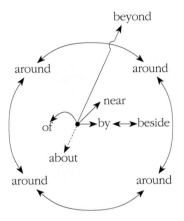

(1) One **of** us will receive the president award.

우리 중 한 명이 회장상을 받을 것이다.

(2) She sat **by** the fire.

그는 난로 가에 앉았다.

(3) We live **near** the beach.

우리는 해변 가에 산다.

(4) She sat **beside** me.

그녀는 내 옆에 나란히 앉았다.

(5) The earth go **(a)round** the sun.

지구는 태양의 둘레를 돈다.

(6) The papers were scattered **about** the room.

신문들이 방 여기저기에 흩어져 있다.

(7) Wednesday is **between** Tuesday and Thursday.

수요일은 화요일과 목요일 사이에 있다.

(8) The movie star is **among** the crowd now.

그 영화배우는 지금 혼잡한 군중 사이에 있다.

(9) He lives **beyond** the river.

그는 강 건너에 산다.

실전문제

09 There are some similarities in the qualifications of two applicants, but the differences _____ them are wide.

(A) among   (B) between   (C) of   (D) on

10 The international food fair held on April 8, offered various food from all _____ the world free of charge.

(A) of   (B) through   (C) around   (D) about

11 Our union leader was defeated by the rival candidate _____ a margin of about 100 votes.

(A) by   (B) in   (C) to   (D) on

12 All full-time staff are eligible to participate in the revised health plan, which will become effective from the first _____ the month.

(A) of   (B) to   (C) from   (D) for

4) 방법 전치사

시간 전치사와 **장소** 전치사를 **제외**한 모든 **전치사**를 말한다.

(1) He was killed **by** the enemy.
그는 적에 의해서 죽임을 당했다.

(2) We had an accident **because of** the rain.
우리는 비 때문에 사고를 당했다.

(3) His failure resulted **from** his laziness.

그의 실수는 그의 게으름에 기인한다.

(4) I'm working **for** money.

나는 지금 돈 때문에 일하고 있는 중이다.

(5) The accounting manager made a long address **on** accounting.

경리 부장님께서 회계에 대한 일장연설을 하셨다.

(6) Be patient **with** the employees.

직원들에 대해 인내심을 가져 주세요.

실전문제

13 All sewing was actually done _____ hand until the invention of the sewing machine in the eighteenth century.

(A) over   (B) with   (C) by   (D) on

14 The company audit informed us that the fault discovered during the routine check resulted _____ all staff's carelessness.

(A) in   (B) for   (C) from   (D) with

15 The position is most suited for a job seekers with a passion _____ sales management and customer acquisition.

(A) by   (B) of   (C) for   (D) to

16 _____ the rapid spread of railways and the air flights, long-distance traveling became more common than ever.

(A) In   (B) For   (C) With   (D) At

(7) He is a worker **of** courage.
그는 용기 있는 일꾼이다.

(8) He went to work **in spite of** his cold.
그는 감기에도 불구하고 직장에 나갔다.

(9) He joined the meeting **wit**h his secretary.
그는 비서와 함께 모임에 참석했다.

(10) We exchanged products **for** bread.
우리는 제품을 빵과 바꿔 먹었다.

 실전문제

17 People see our advertisements repeatedly and feel a sense _____ friendliness so much that they buy our goods.

(A) along   (B) in   (C) of   (D) on

18 Our company couldn't increase the production capacity due to the regulations _____ high demand from customers,

(A) in spite   (B) in despite of   (C) despite of   (D) in spite of

19 Most employees feel it dangerous not to conform _____ the rules of the regulations amended by the new management.

(A) to   (B) in   (C) for   (D) on

20 In the late 1940s, television first began to seriously compete _____ radio for audiences and advertisers.

(A) for   (B) with   (C) to   (D) at

5) 시간 전치사

(1) 짧은, 중간, 긴 시간의 at, on, in, 시간 경과의 in

The shop opens **at** 10 a.m. at the weekend.
가게는 주말에는 오전 10시에 엽니다.

I watch TV only **on** weekdays.
저는 주중에만 TV를 시청합니다.

He was born **in** May **in** 1995.
그는 1995년 5월에 태어났다.

I will be back **in** ten minutes.
10분이 지나면 돌아오겠다.

(2) –동안의 for, during, over, through

I stayed there **for** 10 days.
거기에 10일 동안 머물렀다.

We visited there **during** the company vacation.
우리는 회사 휴가 중에 거기를 방문했다.

We enjoyed gambling **over** the holidays.
우리는 휴일 내내 도박을 즐겼다.

We stayed at the casino **through** the night.
우리는 밤새도록 카지노에 있었다.

(3) –전, 후, 부터, 까지의 before, after, from, by, till, until

All employees should be back **by** 6 to attend the meeting.
모든 직원들은 미팅에 참석하러 6시 까지는 들어와야 한다.

Stay here **till** lunch time.
점심 때 까지는 여기에 머물러 있어야 한다.

실전문제

21 The CEO of Apple Inc, Steve Jobs was born at San Francisco in February 24, 1955 _____ 3:30 in the afternoon.

(A) on   (B) at   (C) on   (D) in

22 Ms. Csupo said that she would return to work at least before Wednesday, but she didn't come back _____ Friday.

(A) at   (B) until   (C) in   (D) on

23 _____ the promotion campaign, a 10% discount will apply on all orders received before April 10th.

(A) As   (B) When   (C) While   (D) During

24 Vigo began looking for the document _____ the night but he couldn't find it till next morning.

(A) on   (B) through   (C) to   (D) in

3 행사 어휘 연구

1) **attend** v. 참석하다; n. **attendance** 출석, 참석

   ex: 회의에 참석하다.

2) **presentation** n. 발표; v. **present** 보여주다, 수여하다, 참석하다

   ex: 신제품에 관한 발표회가 있다.

3) **address** n. 연설, 주소; v. 연설하다, 주소를 쓰다

　　ex: 직원들에게 연설을 하다.

4) **complete** v. 작성하다; n. **completion**^(매매) 실현, 완료, 완성

　　ex: 지원서를 작성하다.

5) **approval** n. 승인, 결재; v. **approve** 승인하다

　　ex: 최종 승인을 받다.

6) **outline** n. 개요, 윤곽, 요강; v. 윤곽을 보여주다, 개요를 말하다

　　ex: 발표의 요지를 요약하다.

실전문제

25　Human resources department should ＿＿＿＿＿＿ all new employee training programs before they start their works.

　　(A) complete　　　　　　(B) approve
　　(C) consent　　　　　　(D) settle

26　Team members should not make any private vacation plans before they receive ＿＿＿＿＿＿ from their team leader.

　　(A) admission　　　　　(B) approval
　　(C) allowance　　　　　(D) appreciation

4 독해 연구

Watch Warranty

Warranty coverage. This watch is warranted to be free of defective materials or workmanship. This warranty does not cover the strap or batteries, or wear on the case or lens. This warranty is void if the watch has been damaged by accident, unreasonable use, neglect, improper service or other causes not arising out of defects in material or workmanship.

Warranty performance. During the above one year warranty period your watch will either be repaired or replaced with a reconditioned model of an equivalent quality when the watch is returned with a $3.00 handling fee, postage prepaid and insured to: Worldly Time Inc. P.O. Box 1111 Tako, U.S.A. 61234

In the event of replacement with a reconditioned model, the replacement unit will continue the warranty of the original watch or 90 days, whichever is longer. Other than the $3.00 handling fee, postage and insurance requirement, no charge will be made for such repair, adjustment and/or replacement. After 1 year current repair rates will also be charged.

 실전문제

27 This warranty covers?

    (A) the lens.   (B) defects in materials.

    (C) damage by accident.   (D) all of the above.

28 To get your watch repaired at the company's expense, you have to?

(A) pay a $3.00 handling fee.
(B) send it in within a year.
(C) pay the return postage.
(D) all of the above.

29 If you bought your watch on Feb. 1st and sent it to be repaired on Aug. 1st, the warranty on the reconditioned model would be?

(A) one year.   (B) 90 days.
(C) 6 months.   (D) none of the above.

30 What is the meaning of the word 'warranty'?

(A) promise   (B) contract
(C) guarantee   (D) pledge

TOEIC Extended

PART
03

TOEIC Extended

구문 편

CHAPTER
10

준동사
(부정사·동명사·분사)

동사에 to나 −ing, 또는 −ed를 붙이면 **부정사, 동명사, 분사**가 되는데 이를 **준동사**라고 부른다. 준동사는 **명사**나 **형용사, 부사 자리**에 온다.

1 부정사

동사 앞에 to을 붙인 '**to+동사**'를 **부정사**라고 부른다. 부정사는 문장 속에 쓰이기 전에는 어떤 품사인지 알 수 없다 그래서 **정해지지 않은 품사**^(=부정사)라고 부른다. 이 부정사가 문장 속에서 **명사 자리**에 들어가면 **명사, 형용사 자리**에 들어가면 **형용사, 부사 자리**에 들어가면 **부사**로 쓰인다.

1) 명사로 쓰이는 경우

(1) 부정사가 주어가 된다.

To succeed in business world is not easy.
사업계에서 성공하는 것은 쉽지가 않다.

(2) 부정사가 목적어가 된다.

My graduates want **to be** a hotelier at a big hotel.
내 졸업생들은 큰 호텔의 호텔리어가 되고 싶어 한다.

We plan **to open** a new branch in Hongkong next year.
우리 회사 내년에 홍콩 지사를 개설할 예정이다.

동사 예 : want(-을 원하다), plan(-을 계획하다), wish(-을 소원하다), decide(-을 결정하다), offer(-을 제공하다), promise(-을 약속하다), agree(-을 동의하다), fail(-을 실패하다), ask(-을 묻다), expect(-을 기대하다), choose(-을 선택하다), help(-을 돕다)

실전문제

01 In response to your request for a 20% discount for the new item, we regret _____ that we cannot offer more than 15%.

(A) saying   (B) to say

(C) to have said   (D) having said

02 More people are planning to try _____ smoking, because they are afraid that it may be harmful to their body.

(A) stopping   (B) to stop

(C) stop   (D) to stopping

03 It becoming more and more important for employees to know _____ a computer than ever before.

(A) how to use   (B) using   (C) to use   (D) how using

04 I had hoped _____ French but I did not have any extra money to take a course at a private educational institute.

(A) learn   (B) to learn   (C) learned   (D) learning

(3) 부정사가 주격 보어가 된다.

The team manager's duty is **to supervise** the team members.
팀장의 의무는 팀원들을 감독하는 것이다.

We are **to be married** next month.
우리 다음 달에 결혼하게 됩니다.

(4) 부정사가 목적격 보어가 된다.

The supervisor enforced us **to work** overtime.
상사는 우리에게 야근을 하게 했다.

The president told me not **to work** overtime.
사장님은 야근하지 말라도 말씀하셨다.

동사 예 : enforce(A에게 B를 강요하다), tell(A에게 B를 말하다), advise(A에게 B를 충
고하다), remind(A에게 B를 상기하다), encourage(A에게 B를 격려하다),
persuade(A에게 B를 설득하다), want(A에게 B를 원하다), ask(A에게 B를 요
구하다), expect(A에게 B를 기대하다), choose(A에게 B를 선택하다), help(A
에게 B를 도와주다)

실전문제

05 The purpose of this survey is _____ how much the customers know about the dedication of our customer service representatives.

(A) finding out   (B) to find out
(C) to finding out   (D) find out

06 The business man suffered heavy losses which forced him _____ his business and all his assets.

(A) giving up   (B) to give up
(C) to giving up   (D) give up

07 The executives reminded us _____ only the best companies in terms of investment opportunities.

(A) to watch   (B) watching

(C) watch   (D) watched

08 Nobody would object to our inviting the team manager _____ us to the employee' birthday party.

(A) join   (B) joining   (C) to join   (D) to joining

2) 형용사로 쓰이는 경우

부정사가 앞의 **명사**를 **수식**한다.

He always has a good idea **to introduce** to us.
그는 우리에게 소개할 좋은 아이디어가 하나 있다.

I have a good news **to tell** all employees.
전 직원들에게 할 좋은 소식이 있다.

실전문제

09 The company truck driver quickly stepped on the brake, and the truck came to a stop just in time _____ an accident.

(A) avoiding   (B) avoid   (C) to avoid   (D) to avoiding

10 The accounting department is now searching for the best way _____ the ongoing salary and benefits package for employees.

(A) to improve   (B) improve   (C) improving   (D) to improving

11 The gift package I got from the department store includes tickets for balcony seats _____ the opera *La Boheme*.

(A) to see   (B) seeing   (C) for seeing   (D) see

12 The executive assistant uses a time-management chart _____ how much time she should spend on each project.

(A) in determination   (B) determines

(C) to determine   (D) determination of

3) 부사로 쓰이는 경우

(1) 부정사가 동사를 수식한다.

We came to the personnel department **to submit** our resumes.
우리는 이력서를 제출하기 위해서 인사과에 갔다.

(2) 부정사가 형용사를 수식한다.

The employee was glad **to help** the new president.
직원은 새 회장님을 돕게 되어서 기뻤다.

(3) 부정사가 문장을 수식한다.

To help the charity, we made a donation.
우리는 자선 단체를 돕기 위해서 기부를 했다

실전문제

13 Since the free market economic theory is seen as the best one, economists feel free _____ it to their countries.

(A) to recommend   (B) of recommending

(C) recommending   (D) to recommending

14 Our shop is pleased _____ you that the item you ordered has just arrived, and therefore visit us as soon as possible.

(A) to informing   (B) inform

(C) informing   (D) to inform

2 동명사

동사 뒤에 **-ing**를 붙여 만든 **명사**를 **동명사**라 한다. 문장 속에서도 명사자리에만 쓰인다.

1) 명사로 쓰임

(1) 동명사가 주어로 쓰인다.

Talking with customers is service representatives's job.
고객과 상담하는 것이 서비스 담당 직원의 일이다.

(2) 동명사가 주격 보어로 쓰인다.

His hobby is **discussing** business with clients.
그의 취미는 고객과 사업에 대해 이야기 하는 것이다.

(3) 동명사가 동사의 목적어로 쓰인다.

The team manager enjoys **talking** with his team members.
팀장님은 팀원들과 얘기하는 것을 즐기신다.

I finished **completing** the job application form.
입사 지원서 작성을 끝냈다.

동사 예 : enjoy(-을 즐기다), finish(-을 끝내다), quit(-을 떠나다), consider(-을 고려하다), suggest(-을 제안하다), avoid(-을 피하다), give up(-을 포기하다), postpone(-을 연기하다), recommend(-을 추천하다)

실전문제

15 _____ accurate records about sales figures has never been questioned by anyone in the accounting department.

(A) His keeping (B) Him to keep

(C) Him keeping (D) His to keep

16 Our good service and quality goods are main reasons why customers enjoy _____ business with us.

(A) doing (B) having (C) to do (D) to have

17 The government should consider _____ the same actions to drinking as it does to smoking.

(A) took (B) take (C) taking (D) to take

18 I regretted not _____ N.Y. branch manager position, where I could send my two kids to universities there.

(A) to accept (B) accepting

(C) accepted (D) to have accepted

(4) 동명사가 전치사의 목적어로 쓰인다.

You can learn accounting more by **attending** the seminar.
세미나를 통해 회계를 더 배울 수 있다.

He is also extremely interested in **attending** business meeting.
그는 또한 비즈니스 모임에 참석하는 데에 관심이 지대합니다.

실전문제

19 Upon _____ the survey form, I received a gift certificate for a free pizza and a sweatshirt from a local restaurant.

(A) complete   (B) completing   (C) to complete   (D) completion

20 The Korean government did not approve of _____ in Korea since she rebelled against the country.

(A) she staying   (B) her to stay   (C) her staying   (D) her stayed

3 분사

동사 뒤에 **−ing**를 붙이면 **현재분사**가, **동사** 뒤에 **−ed**를 붙이면 **과거분사**가 된다.

※ **동명사에 붙은 −ing**와 **현재분사에 붙은 −ing**는 서로 다른 것이다. 철자부터 달랐던 것이 역사적인 변화의 과정에서 같은 형이 되었을 뿐 **서로 아무런 관계가 없다.**

1) 현재분사와 과거분사의 구분

(1) 현재분사는 능동적 의미를, 과거분사는 수동적 의미를 나타낸다.

The worker **working** in the garden is a new comer.(능동)
정원에서 일하고 있는 인부는 신참내기다.

The **broken** window is not up to the child but up to his parents.(수동)
깨진 창문은 그 아이가 아니라 아이 부모의 책임이다.

(2) 현재분사는 진행적 의미를, 과거분사는 완료적 의미를 나타낸다.

The clerk is **reading** a document.(진행)
그 점원은 서류를 읽고 있다.

All the leaves have **fallen**.(완료)
모든 잎들이 떨어졌다.

2) 분사의 형용사로 쓰임

(1) 분사가 주격 보어로 쓰인다.

All the employees felt **confused** for the president's resignation.
회장님의 사임에 모든 직원들이 혼란스러워졌다.

(2) 분사가 목적격 보어로 쓰인다.

The supervisor made the regulation **abolished**.
상사는 그 규정을 폐기시켜 버렸다.

(3) 분사가 앞의 명사를 수식한다.

We are the company **manufacturing** the goods.
우리가 바로 그 상품을 생산하는 공장이다.

(4) 분사가 뒤의 명사를 수식한다.

The manager gave us a very **confusing** manual.
팀장님께서 우리에게 매우 혼란스러운 매뉴얼을 주셨다.

 실전문제

21 Understanding the cultural habits of another nation is a complex, _____ task but the rewards are enormous.

(A) bewildered (B) bewildering
(C) bewilder (D) to bewilder

22 The employees _____ should seek after no other benefits, for there can be no greater benefit than a good salary.

(A) well paying (B) who pay well
(C) well paid (D) who is paid well

23 The customer service representatives have been doing their best to keep the investors _____ of the market conditions.

(A) informing (B) inform
(C) informed (D) information

24 A free watch will be provided with every purchase of $ 20.00 or more for a _____ period of time.

(A) limit (B) limits (C) limited (D) limiting

3) 분사의 부사로 쓰임(=분사구문)

접속사+주어+동사로 되어 있는 부사절에서 **접속사, 주어**를 **생략**하고 동사에 **-ing**를 붙여 만든 **현재분사**로 시작하는 문장을 **분사구문**이라 한다.

(1) 시간 : -할 때, -한 후에, -하는 동안

Putting down the newspaper, the manager went out.(=After he put down-)
팀장님은 신문을 내려놓고 나서 나가셨다.

(2) 이유 : -이기 때문에, -이므로

Using international suppliers, our company got cheaper prices.(=As it used-)
우리 회사는 국제적인 납품업자를 이용하기 때문에 가격이 저렴합니다.

(3) 동시상황 : -하면서 동시에

Dining together, we discussed the contract.(=As we dined-)
우리는 식사를 함께 하면서, 계약에 대해서 이야기 했다.

125

실전문제

25 _____ a second time, he looked forward to a new term focused on domestic rather than foreign operations.

(A) Being inaugurated   (B) Inaugurating
(C) Inaugurate   (D) Inauguration

26 The weather _____, the participants as well as the company enjoyed the outdoor launch presentation.

(A) was improved   (B) improving
(C) having improved   (D) has improved

4 시사 어휘 연구

1) **publish** v. 출판하다, 발행하다; n. **publication** 출판, 출판물
   ex: 회사 소식지를 발행하다.

2) **forecast** v. 예보하다, 예측하다; s. predict
   ex: 내일 날씨를 예보하다.

3) **indicator** n. 지표, (속도, 입력)계; v. **indicate** 지시하다, 나타내다
   ex: 기름이 없음을 나타내다.

4) **conservation** n. 보호, 보존; v. **conserve** 보호하다, 보존하다
   ex: 자연을 보호하다.

5) **security** n. 보안, 경비; v. **secure** 보호하다
   ex: 보안요원을 부르다.

6) **recognition** n. 인정, 인식, 표창; v. **recognize** 인정하다, 깨닫다

ex: 업적을 인정하다.

실전문제

27 CCTV cameras have been set up for _____ reasons in front ot the four main gates of the office buildings.

(A) security　　(B) predict　　(C) traffic　　(D) illumination

28 They say that the new president have gained international _____ for her excellent performance at an NGO.

(A) recognition　(B) shame　　(C) name　　(D) issue

5 독해 연구

Cabin Rental Regulation

1. Each cabin has a kitchen with a sink and refrigerator.
2. Each cabin is equipped with the necessary dishes, working utensils and silver ware.
3. Occupants of cabins must furnish bed linens, blankets, pillows and all consumable products.
4. Cabins will be checked by the Property Manager prior to occupancy and at the close of each occupancy. The cabin deposit may be retained to cover breakage or damage to the cabin or for cleaning in the event

the cabin is not released in a satisfactory condition.

5. Property Manager reserves the right to reject any application or evict any person or group of persons for failure to conform with park regulations. Cabins are subject to inspection at all times. It is expected that cabin guests will be quiet in the cabin after 11:00 p.m.

6. No outside fires are permitted in family cabin area.

 실전문제

29 The property manager?

    (A) will insect the cabin when you leave.

    (B) cannot enter your cabin.

    (C) will turn out all lights at 11:00

    (D) will help you build a fire if you want one.

30 If you break the park regulations?

    (A) you can be asked to leave.

    (B) you will lose your deposit.

    (C) you will have to clean the cabin.

    (D) you will be expected to stay in your cabin after 11:00.

CHAPTER 11

비교문

형용사나 **부사**가 자기들의 **성질·수량·양태**의 **정도**를 **견주어** 보는 것을 **비교**라 한다.

1 원급에 의한 비교

A와 B는 -에 있어서 '**양쪽이 같다**', '**같지 않다**', 또는 한 쪽에 얼마를 '**접어주면 양 쪽이 같다**'는 식으로 비교하는 것을 **원급 비교**라 한다.

1) 동등비교

She is as old as he.
그녀와 그는 나이에 있어서 같다.

My dress is the same color as yours.
내 드레스 색깔은 네 것과 같다.

2) 차등 비교

He is not as/so old as she.
그는 그녀와 나이가 같지 않다.

I am twice as heavy as he.
그의 몸무게에 두 배하면 내 몸무게와 같다.

실전문제

01 Since the current marketing strategy is not the same efficient one _____ the old one, heavy losses are expected.

(A) as   (B) to   (C) than   (D) so

02 The Zero Gravity Pen was developed by a manufacturer who used as precise measurements _____ those used in spacecraft.

(A) as   (B) the same   (C) so   (D) to

03 California will save _____ 90 million dollars a year if they keep the death penalty which they're campaigning against.

(A) as possible as   (B) as many as
(C) as soon as   (D) as much as

04 The boss raises hell to the staff for working too slowly, even though they're working _____ they can.

(A) as quick as   (B) as fast as
(C) as possible as   (D) as fastly as

2 비교급에 의한 비교

A는 B보다 -에 있어서 '**더 -하다**', '**덜 -하다**' 는 식으로 비교하는 것을 **비교급 비교**라 한다.

1) 영어식 비교

-er than을 사용한다.

John is taller **than** I.
John은 나보다 더 크다.

He is poorer **than** I.
그는 나보다 더 가난하다.

2) 불어식 비교

more ~ than, less ~ than을 사용한다.

She is **more** careful **than** I.
그녀는 나보다 더 조심성이 있다.

He is **less** talkative **than** she.
그는 그녀보다 덜 말이 많다.

3) 라틴어식 비교

-or to를 사용한다.

She is juni**or to** him.
그녀는 그보다 손아래이다.

He is inferi**or to** me in English.
그는 영어에 있어서 그보다 못하다.

4) 변형된 비교급

The more one has, **the more** he wants.
인간은 가지면 가질 수 록 더 원한다.

He works **all the harder as** he needs more money.
그는 더 많은 돈이 필요하기 때문에 더욱더 열심히 일을 한다.

실전문제

05 According to the recent report about marriage, the average age of marriage is getting _____ than last year.

(A) higher   (B) highest   (C) high   (D) more high

06 Thanks to the new photographic printing techniques, the cost of book publishing will be _____ expensive than before.

(A) less   (B) more   (C) less   (D) more

07 The marketing director knows more about marketing and sales strategies _____ anyone else.

(A) than   (B) as   (C) so   (D) to

08 As sales were _____ consistent than before, the president ordered his staff to scale down the production.

(A) far less   (B) more   (C) very   (D) a little

3 최상급에 의한 비교

모든 대상에서, 모든 장소에서, 모든 시간에서 최고인 것을, **the+최상급 ～ of/in/ever**를 사용하여 비교하는 것을 **최상급 비교**라 한다.

1) 최상급+of 사람(사물)

Health is **the most** precious **of** all.
건강이 든 것 중에서 가장 중요하다.

2) 최상급+in+장소

Health is **the most** precious **in** the world.
건강이 세상에서 가장 중요하다.

3) 최상급+ever(시간)

His sales record is **the best** one that has **ever** been made.
그의 판매 기록이 이제까지 만들어진 가장 좋은 기록이다.

 ## 실전문제

09 O'Hare Airport in Chicago handles more passengers, freight
and mail traffics than _____ in America.

(A) any airports   (B) any other airport
(C) any other airports   (D) any airport

10 Michael Jackson's album "Thriller" was the most successful
album _____ recorded in terms of sales.

(A) as   (B) ever   (C) being   (D) was

11 Amsterdam Farmers Market on the 7the Street serves the
_____ roses and tulips in this city.

(A) good   (B) better   (C) bad   (D) best

12 Of all company's club activities the sales manager likes
fishing _____ , but he does not go fishing very often.

(A) best   (B) good   (C) better   (D) lest

4 조직 어휘 연구

1) **conference** n. 총회, 학회; v. **confer** 협의하다, 수여하다
   ex: 기자 회견이 열리다.

2) **conventional** a. 관습적인, 관례적이; n. **convention** 관습, 대회, 총회
   ex: 컨벤션 센터는 주차장이 넓다.

3) **constitute** v. 구성하다, 제정하다; n. **constitution** 구조, 헌법
   ex: 이사회 멤버를 구성하다.

4) **institution** n. 기관, 협회; v. **institute** (제도, 정책을) 도입하다
   ex: 기술연수원을 열다.

5) **conflict** n. 갈등, 충돌; s. **argument** 논쟁, 갈등, 충돌
   ex: 노사 갈등이 있다.

6) **reputation** n. 명성, 명판; a. **reputational** 평판이 좋은; s. **renown** 평판, 명성
   ex: 명성을 얻다.

 실전문제

13 The government is trying to resolve the _____ about salary reduction existing between the management ant the labor union.

(A) recognition   (B) conflict
(C) fight   (D) competition

14   The sales manager has gained a _____ for perfect dealing the customer complaints coming from local areas as well as down town.

(A) reputation   (B) popularism   (C) fame   (D) popularity

5 독해 연구

Recreational Vehicles

Recreational vehicles(=RVs) are back on the road. As families search for affordable vacations and gas prices are lower than ever, many people are rediscovering the Winnebagos of their youth. Meanwhile the recreational vehicle industry is prospering. Last year it sold 254,500 units - one of its best years ever.

The image of RVs and their owners is changing rapidly. RVs were once the vacation transportation for retired folks who found the modest campers an inexpensive way to see the country. But today's younger travelers have more exclusive tastes. RV parks with country-club style amenities like golf courses and health clubs cater to the new style camper.

Fleetwood the world's largest manufacturer of RVs, recently introduced a sport utility trailer with a back that folds down to become a loading ramp for personal watercraft or snowmobiles. The trailer, and the rest of Fleetwood's new models, are prewired for satellite television. Seems like the great outdoors is even greater when you've got a little luxury.

실전문제

15 What is a good title for this article?

(A) "Young People Finally Get Away from TV"
(B) "RVs Are Back and Better Than Ever "
(C) "Snowmobiles Can Come Along Too"
(D) "Retired Folks Get Off the Road"

16 How have RVs changed in recent years?

(A) They're more elaborate.
(B) They're more affordable.
(C) They're more compact.
(D) They're less complicated.

17 According to the article, the increased popularity of traveling by RV has resulted in which of the following?

(A) Overcrowded parks
(B) Less interest in technology
(C) More people playing golf and going to health clubs
(D) Higher sales of RVs

18 What is the meaning of the word 'utility'?

(A) benefit   (B) convenience
(C) usefulness   (D) efficacy

CHAPTER
12

수동태

'철수가 회사를 만들었다'는 표현이 '회사는 철수에 의해서 만들어져 있다'는 표현으로 바뀌는 것 즉, '**만들다**'는 **동작** 표현이 '**만들어져 있다**'는 **상태** 표현으로 바뀌는 것을 **수동태**라 한다.

1 수동태 만들기

1) 능동문의 **주어**는 수동문의 **by**의 **목적어**로 간다.
2) 능동문의 **동사**는 수동문의 **be와 −ed 사이**로 간다.
3) 능동문의 **목적어**는 수동문의 **주어**로 간다.

The team leader loves his team members.

His team members are loved by the team leader.

2 3형식의 수동태

동작, 경험 동사 문장은 **수동이 가능**하나, **소유, 상태 동사 문장**은 **수동이 불가능**하다.

1) 동작 · 경험 동사의 수동태

I **completed** the application.
나는 지원서를 작성했다.

→ The application **was completed by** me.
지원서는 나에 의해 작성되어 있다.

Tom **heard** the music.
Tom은 음악을 들었다.

→ The music **was heard by** Tom.
음악이 Tom에게 들렸다.

2) 소유 · 상태 동사의 수동태

The new president **resembles** his father.
새 회장님은 아버님을 닮았다.

→ ※ His father **is resembled by** the new president.^(※은 틀린 문장 표시)
새 회장님의 아버님을 닮았다.

3 4형식 문장의 수동태

목적어가 두 개라 **두 개의 수동태가 가능**하다.

1) 간접 목적어를 주어로 하는 수동태

The company gave **all staff** a special bonus.
회사는 전 직원에게 특별 보너스를 주었다.

→ **All staff** were given a special bonus by the company.
모든 직원에게 특별 보너스가 회사에 의해서 주어졌다.

2) 직접 목적어를 주어로 하는 수동태

The company gave all staff **a special bonus**.
회사는 전 직원에게 특별 보너스를 주었다.

→ **A special bonus** was given to all staff by the company.
특별 보너스가 회사에 의해서 모든 직원에게 주어졌다.

동사 예 : give(to)(A에게 B를 주다), offer(to)(A에게 B를 제공해 주다), send(to)(A에게 B를 보내주다), ask(of)(A에게 B를 요청하다)

 실전문제

01 Most of the package tour tourists wonder how long ago this beautiful Ulm Cathedral, the tallest in the world _____.

(A) was built   (B) had built
(C) has built   (D) is built

02 The need for the Korean economy to gain ground on the world market _____ more acutely now than ever before.

(A) will feel   (B) have felt
(C) was being felt   (D) is being felt

03 When we _____ that there would be an hour-wait, we had no choice but to try to head for another restaurant.

(A) were told   (B) was told
(C) are told   (D) is told

04 Since the air-conditioner was found to be not as effective as the manual claimed, it _____ by its repairman right now.

(A) is repairing   (B) repairs
(C) is being repaired   (D) has repaired

4 5형식 문장의 수동태

1) 목적격 보어가 명사일 때

The employees call him **the president**.
직원들은 그를 회장님이라고 부른다.

→ He was called **the president** by the employees.
그는 직원들에 의해 회장님이라고 불린다.

2) 목적격 보어가 형용사 일 때

Customers consider the company **reliable**.
고객들은 그 회사가 믿을 만 하다고 여긴다.

→ The company is considered **reliable** by the customers.
회사는 고객들에 의해 믿을 만 하다고 여겨지고 있다.

 실전문제

05 Though the director sometimes does not even lift a finger, he
_____ as efficient as other workers.

(A) considers   (B) is considered
(C) are considered   (D) is considering

06 When I got to the airport, the airplane had been delayed, so
he _____ to be an hour late.

(A) was expected   (B) is expected
(C) expected   (D) expect

⑤ By가 변형된 수동태

대부분의 수동 문장은 뒤에 **행위자**가 오기 때문에, 행위자를 나타내는 전치사 **by**가 쓰이지만, 일부 수동 문장에서는 행위자 대신에 **원인, 도구, 대상, 관계**를 나타내는 것이 나오기도 한다. 이때는 by 대신에 **at, with, about, to**등으로 바꾸어 쓴다.

1) at+원인

I was frightened **at** the news.
뉴스에 놀랐다.

He is very much pleased **at** what I did.
그는 내가 말한 것에 무척 기뻤다.

2) with+도구

The mountain was covered **with** snow.
산은 눈으로 덮혀 있다.

The manager will satisfied **with** my report.
팀장님은 내 보고서에 만족하실 것이다.

3) about+대상

He is concerned **about** my business.
그는 내 사업에 관심이 있다.

The worker is worried **about** his job much.
그 노동자는 자기 일에 걱정이 많다.

4) to+관계

I was married **to** the president's daughter.
나는 회장 따님과 결혼했다.

The president is dedicated **to** his employees.
회장님은 그의 직원들에게 헌신한다.

실전문제

07 If you are chosen _____ a successful candidate for the job, you will receive a congratulatory notice and interview schedule.

   (A) as   (B) by   (C) with   (D) to

08 The organization is composed _____ a group of elected board members and a group of voting membership.

   (A) with   (B) by   (C) of   (D) in

09 Famous for her role in the hit television series, Lost, the actress got married _____ a film producer on March 28.

   (A) by   (B) to   (C) with   (D) in

10 The numerous manufacturing establishments in the Northern States in America, were devoted _____ the grinding of grain.

   (A) to   (B) by   (C) of   (D) for

6 거래 어휘 연구

1) **compete** v. 경쟁하다; n. **competition** 경쟁

   ex: 경쟁사와 경쟁하다.

2) **customized** a. 맞춤형의; v. **customize** 맞춤제작하다

   ex: 옷 한 벌을 맞춤제작하다.

3) **consumption** n. 소비^(품); v. **consume** 소비하다

   ex: 시간은 다 써버리다.

4) **enhance** v. 향상시키다; n. **enhancement** 향상, 개선

   ex: 직원 복지를 향상시키다.

5) **corporation** n. ^(대)기업, 회사; a. **corporate** 회사의, 기업의

   ex: 회사 정책에 반대하다.

6) **estimate** v. 추정하다; n. 추정, 추정치, 견적, 견적서

   ex: 세 개의 견적서를 받다.

실전문제

11 According to a survey study on the energy _____ in Seoul, last year Seoul's power consumption reached its peak.

   (A) recognition   (B) consumption

   (C) spending   (D) use

12 Company economic advisor _____ the firm's foreign investment profit will be $ 1 million in the last quarter of this year.

   (A) indicate   (B) suppose

   (C) estimate   (D) show

7 독해 연구

POSCO

(1)

POSCO posted a net profit of 1.1 trillion won ($1.2 billion) on sales of 5.8 trillion won in the second quarter of the year. Although the company's second-quarter total sales increased by a relatively small 2 percent from the previous quarter, the steel giant's quarterly net profit shot up by 13.3 percent, or 131 billion won.

The steelmaker said that increases in the sales of steel plates for automobiles, and cost saving programs contributed to increasing profits.

(2)

Local manufacturers are looking to revise up sales targets and expand facilities on the back of the economic recovery and brisk exports.

Exports, which account for around 40 percent of the nation's total output, have been fast growing despite the rising won in recent months, posting a record high of $32 billion in June alone. Consumer spending also rose over 6 percent year-on-year in May, reflecting resilient domestic demand.

 실전문제

13   What contributed to increasing profit?

(A) oil price   (B) currency
(C) cost-saving programs   (D) people

14 What is true about national economy?

(A) 40 percent of total output is exports.

(B) Exports have been slowly growing.

(C) consumer spending has decreased.

(D) Situation is bad.

15 What can be said about the manufacturing companies?

(A) Sales and profit are declining.

(B) It is a tough time.

(C) Manufacturing industries are showing exceptional growth.

(D) They are about the same.

16 What is the meaning of the word 'resilient'?

(A) recoverable   (B) smooth

(C) slippy   (D) residential

CHAPTER
13

가정법

실제 일어났거나 일어나고 있는 일을 실제 시제로 표현한 것을 직설법이라 한다.
실제로 일어나지 않았거나 일어날 가능성이 없는 일을 **가정해서**, 시제를 달리하여
표현한 것을 **가정법**^(=가짜 문장)이라 한다.

※ 직설법과 가정법 구분

(1) 직설법 : 진짜 문장

If I **have** time, I **will** help you now.^(시간이 있나 없나 따져 봐야 함)
지금 내가 시간이 있으면 너를 도와 줄 수가 있다.

(2) 가정법 : 가짜 문장

If I **had** time, I **would** help you now.^(시간이 없음)
지금 시간이 있으면 너를 도와 줄 수가 있을 텐데.(시간이 없어 도와줄 수 없음)

1 가정법 과거

현재 사실에 **반대**되는 것을 **가정** 할 때 쓴다.

1) 가정법 기본형

If+주어+동사의 과거형~, 주어+조동사의 과거형~.

(지금) ~한다면, ~해 줄 수 있을 텐데.

If I **knew** the best restaurant, I **would** recommend the restaurant to you.
내가 최고로 좋은 식당을 안다면 네게 추천해줄 수 있을 텐데.

If I **were** you, I **would** not make such a mistake.
내가 너라면 그런 실수는 않 했을 텐데.

 ## 실전문제

01 It would be good if you _____ be here, but it is not
essential that you be included in the teleconference.

(A) can   (B) were able to

(C) is able to   (D) are to

02 If the company were able to spend all its assets on the advertising
campaign this year, it _____ more customers.

(A) reached   (B) reach

(C) can reach   (D) could reach

2) Time that 형

~time that + 주어 + 동사 과거형~.
(지금) ~해야 할 시간이다.

It's **time** that you **went** to bed now.
너 지금 잠자리 들 시간이다.

3) Would rather 형

~would rather that+주어+동사 과거형~.
나는 주어가 ~하기를 바란다.

I'd **rather** that you **went** back to your country now.
나 네가 지금 고국으로 돌아가기를 바란다.

4) 숙어형

If it were not for~, 주어+조동사의 과거.
~이 없다면, ~할 수 없을 텐데.

If it **were not for** water, nothing **could** live.
물 없이는 아주 것도 살 수 없다.

 실전문제

03 I would rather you _____ anything any more for the time being, since you just recovered from the traffic accident.

(A) do   (B) didn't do   (C) don't   (D) did

04 He was already on the wrong side of thirty and therefore it's about time he _____ a wife and settled down.

(A) finds   (B) should find   (C) found   (D) had found

05 If it were not for our dedicated service team, we _____ not be able to handle so many client firms at the same time.

(A) will   (B) would   (C) were   (D) are

06 Since the employee has to do all office work by herself, she does not wishes she _____ working in a small corporation.

(A) is not   (B) was not   (C) were not   (D) does not

2 가정법 과거완료

과거 사실에 반대되는 것을 **가정**할 때 쓴다.

1) 기본형

If+주어+had+p.p~, 주어+조동사 과거+had+p.p.~.
~했더라면, 주어가 ~을 했었을 텐데.

If I **had known** earlier, I **would have made** a early reservation.
좀 더 일찍 알았더라면, 일찍 예약을 했었을 텐데.

2) 숙어형

If it had not been for/But for/Without~, 주어+조동사 과거-.
~가 없었다면, ~했을 텐데.

If it had not been for your help, I **would have failed**.
네 도움이 없었더라면 난 실패했을 텐데.

실전문제

07 _____ the financial crisis, our company could have earned a much larger profit last year just as we expected.

(A) If
(B) Were it not for
(C) Had it not been for
(D) It has not been for

08 If he had managed to complete the training course, he _____ promoted in his last advancement opportunity.

(A) would have been
(B) will have been
(C) was
(D) had

09 Had _____ not been for the help of all the team members, we would not have succeeded in increasing sales volume.

(A) we   (B) there   (C) it   (D) you

10 If the management had not allowed us to advertise the new products, we _____ not have gathered many customers.

(A) will   (B) would   (C) shall   (D) may

3 가정법 미래

미래에 대한 **실현 가능성이 없는 가정**을 표현한다.

1) 조동사 형

If+주어+should~, 주어+조동사의 과거형~.
~한다면, ~할 텐데.

If our manager s**hould** attend the meeting, we **would** not attend the meeting.
팀장님이 모임에 참석하신다면 우리는 안 참석해도 될 텐데.

2) Were to 형

If+주어+were to~, 주어+조동사의 과거형~.
−한다면, −할 텐데.

If the sun **were to** rise in the west, I **would** marry you.
해가 서쪽에서 뜬다면 너랑 결혼해 줄게.

실전문제

11 If the government _____ increase its education programs, literacy could increase to almost 100%.

(A) shall　　(B) will　　(C) should　　(D) may

12 If you _____ see the employee who made the launch be spoiled, what would you tell him?

(A) were to　　(B) were　　(C) was to　　(D) was

4 가정법 혼합형

1) 시제 혼합형

가정법 과거완료 If절+가정법 과거 주절

If I **had studied** harder before, I **might** get a better job now.
전에 공부를 더 열심히 했었더라면 지금 더 나은 직장을 잡을 수 있을 텐데.

2) 가정법과 직설법 혼합형

가정법 과거완료 주절+but+직설법 문장

I **would have gone** to the concert but I didn't have time.
음악회에 갈 수 있었을 텐데, 그러나 (실제로는) 시간이 없었다.

실전문제

13 If the government had built more homes last year, the housing

problems _____ not be so serious now.

(A) shall   (B) will   (C) would   (D) should

14 Apple, dismantled by the government in 1999, _____

have remained as a trading conglomerate, but it lacked experience.

(A) would   (B) could   (C) should   (D) might

15 Jenny would go to the musical on the premiere now if she

_____ able to get an advanced ticket before.

(A) were   (B) had been
(C) would have been   (D) was

16 The employee might have come to the company in time for

the training session _____ rather late.

(A) if he has gotten up   (B) if he gets up
(C) but he got up   (D) but he gets up

5 사회 어휘 연구

1) **resident** n. 주민, 거주민; v. **reside** 살다, 거주하다

  ex: 거주민들의 수가 늘다.

2) **foundation** n. 재단, 기초, 설립; v. **found** 세우다, 설립하다

  ex: 회사를 하나 세우다.

3) **charity** n. 자선 (단체); a. **charitable** 자선의

ex: 한 자선 단체에 기부하다.

4) **celebrate** v. 축하하다; n. **celebration** 기념, 축하

ex: 진급을 축하하다.

5) **appliance** n. (가정용) 기기, 기구; v. **apply** 적용하다

ex: 가정용 기기를 몇 개 구입하다.

6) **disposal** n. 처리, 처분; v. **dispose** 처리하다, 배치하다

ex: 재고품을 세일로 처리하다.

실전문제

17 As a long-time _____ of Seoul, Mr. Song is familiar with its historical sites and tourist attractions very much.

(A) resident   (B) disposal

(C) appliance   (D) charity

18 The _____ which is scheduled to be delivered on Friday requires installation by a experienced technician.

(A) disposal   (B) appliance

(C) charity   (D) foundation

6 독해 연구

SAMSUNG

(1)

Shinhan Securities analyst agreed to the view that Samsung Electronics Competitiveness is being challenged, especially in DRAM products. "Samsung recently lost to Hynix, in terms of cost reduction in DRAM chips," Chung said. Experts say Samsung's appointment of new heads will positively serve as a new boost to the company's profitability and stock price.

(2)

Samsung's semiconductor business was heavily hurt by a steep drop in the price of memory chips in the second quarter, which forced the company to post 910 billion won in operating profit, the worst figure since the fourth quarter of 2001.

The world's largest memory chip maker said yesterday that Hwang Chang-Kyu, President of semiconductor operations at Samsung Electronics, will be no longer be in charge of the memory business.

 실전문제

19 What can be said about recent status of Samsung Electronics?

(A) They are doing a great job.
(B) Some CEOs have been changed.

(C) Sales have increased slightly.

(D) Some people made mistakes.

20 What is the result of Samsung Electronics' Failure?

(A) They have been some shifts in jobs.

(B) Many workers were fired.

(C) Samsung Electronics edited their objects.

(D) Samsung Electronics is hoping for a objectives.

21 What is the reason for Samsung Electronics' recent failure?

(A) oil price   (B) currency

(C) cost reduction   (D) people

22 What's the meaning of the word 'challenge'?

(A) agree   (B) defy

(C) invite   (D) tackle

TOEIC Extended

PART
04

TOEIC Extended

듣기연습 편

Listening Practice 1

○ PART I

Directions: For each question in this part, you will hear four statements about a picture in your test book. When you hear the statements, you must select the one statement that best describes what you see in the picture. Then find the number of the question on your answer sheet and mark your answer. The statements will not be printed in your test book and will be spoken only one time.

1.

2.

3.

○ PART II

Directions: You will hear a question or statement and three responses spoken in English. They will not be printed in your test book and will be spoken only one time. Select the best response to the question or statement and mark the letter (A), (B), or (C) on your answer sheet.

1. Mark your answer on your answer sheet.

2. Mark your answer on your answer sheet.

3. Mark your answer on your answer sheet.

4. Mark your answer on your answer sheet.

5. Mark your answer on your answer sheet.

6. Mark your answer on your answer sheet.

7. Mark your answer on your answer sheet.

8. Mark your answer on your answer sheet.

● PART Ⅲ

Directions: You will hear some conversation between two people. You will be asked to answer three questions about what the speakers say in each conversation. Select the best response to each question and mark the letter (A), (B), (C), or (D) on your answer sheet. The conversation will not be printed in your test book and wiii be spoken only one time.

1. Where is Ms. Helen now?

   (A) She is outside.
   (B) She is in her office.
   (C) She went back home.
   (D) She went on a trip to Florida.

2. Where is this conversation probably taking place?

   (A) At the airport
   (B) On the phone
   (C) At the hospital
   (D) At the police station

3. What does Mr. Lim imply when he says, "Would you please leave a message?"?

   (A) He is her boss.
   (B) He is quite busy.
   (C) He will do a favor.
   (D) He is going to be out in an hour.

● PART Ⅳ

Directions: You will hear some short talks given by a single speaker, You will be asked to answer three questions about what the speaker says in each short talk. Select the best response to each question and mark the letter (A), (B), (C) or (D) on your answer sheet. The talks will not be printed in your test book and will be spoken only one time.

1. Where was the announcement made?

   (A) In a plane
   (B) In a hospital
   (C) At a clothing shop
   (D) At a doctor's office

2. What is the article you cannot buy in the sky shopping?

   (A) Wine
   (B) Liquor
   (C) Cigarette
   (D) Cosmetics

3. What is the credit card unavailable in the sky shopping?

   (A) VISA
   (B) BC Card
   (C) Master Card
   (D) American Express

Flight #	Destination	Departure Time
KE 923	London	11:00 A.M.
AY 901	Barcelona	2:00 P.M.
7C 203	Seoul	4:00 P.M.
MU 266	Tokyo	7:00 P.M.

4. Where does the speaker most likely work?

   (A) Airport
   (B) Hotel
   (C) Tourist Information Center

(D) Train station

5. Look at the graphic. Which flight is likely to be delayed?

   (A) KE 923

   (B) AY 901

   (C) 7C 203

   (D) MU 266

6. What is recommended for the passengers to do next?

   (A) They may go back to their home.

   (B) They should make contact with accommodation center.

   (C) They should visit information center.

   (D) Information service will be provided online.

Listening Practice 2

⊙ PART I

Directions: For each question in this part, you will hear four statements about a picture in your test book. When you hear the statements, you must select the one statement that best describes what you see in the picture. Then find the number of the question on your answer sheet and mark your answer. The statements will not be printed in your test book and will be spoken only one time.

2.

1.

3.

PART II

Directions: You will hear a question or statement and three responses spoken in English. They will not be printed in your test book and will be spoken only one time. Select the best response to the question or statement and mark the letter (A), (B), or (C) on your answer sheet.

1. Mark your answer on your answer sheet.

2. Mark your answer on your answer sheet.

3. Mark your answer on your answer sheet.

4. Mark your answer on your answer sheet.

5. Mark your answer on your answer sheet.

6. Mark your answer on your answer sheet.

7. Mark your answer on your answer sheet.

8. Mark your answer on your answer sheet.

PART III

Directions: You will hear some conversation between two people. You will be asked to answer three questions about what the speakers say in each conversation. Select the best response to each question and mark the letter (A), (B), (C), or (D) on your answer sheet. The conversation will not be printed in your test book and wiii be spoken only one time.

1. What do the customers think about the price?

   (A) It's very cheap.
   (B) It's very strange.
   (C) It's very expensive.
   (D) It's very reasonable.

2. What are they talking about?

   (A) Potatoes
   (B) A short coat
   (C) Mountain hiking
   (D) Automobile engine

3. What is the price policy of this store?

   (A) the fixed price
   (B) the retail price
   (C) the wholesale price
   (D) the negotiable price

PART IV

Directions: You will hear some short talks given by a single speaker, You will be asked to answer three questions about what the speaker says in each short talk. Select the best response to each question and mark the letter (A), (B), (C) or (D) on your answer sheet. The talks will not be printed in your test book and will be spoken only one time.

1. In non-summer season when do they open Universal Studio?

   (A) At 6:00 o'clock in the morning
   (B) At 7:00 o'clock in the morning
   (C) At 8:00 o'clock in the morning
   (D) At 9:00 o'clock in the morning

2. Which one is not to be experienced in Universal Studio?

   (A) Thrilling shows
   (B) Spine-chilling rides
   (C) Amazing adventures
   (D) Fantastic horse racing

3. What is the world's largest animated figure in Universal Studio?

   (A) Dragon
   (B) Dinosaur
   (C) Elephant
   (D) King Kong

4. What's the main reason to examine food items in the States?

   (A) To check if they are delicious or not.
   (B) To check if they are expensive or not.
   (C) To check if they can be sold out or not.
   (D) To check if they can be brought into the country.

5. How can you get through inspection quicker and avoid fines?

   (A) By cheating agricultural inspectors
   (B) By throwing away some food items
   (C) By concealing agricultural commodities
   (D) By following some declaration guidelines

6. How much is the fine for not declaring food items?

   (A) U$50
   (B) U$70
   (C) U$100
   (D) U$150

Listening Practice 3

○ PART I

Directions: For each question in this part, you will hear four statements about a picture in your test book. When you hear the statements, you must select the one statement that best describes what you see in the picture. Then find the number of the question on your answer sheet and mark your answer. The statements will not be printed in your test book and will be spoken only one time.

1.

2.

3.

○ PART II

Directions: You will hear a question or statement and three responses spoken in English. They will not be printed in your test book and will be spoken only one time. Select the best response to the question or statement and mark the letter (A), (B), or (C) on your answer sheet.

1. Mark your answer on your answer sheet.

2. Mark your answer on your answer sheet.

3. Mark your answer on your answer sheet.

4. Mark your answer on your answer sheet.

5. Mark your answer on your answer sheet.

6. Mark your answer on your answer sheet.

7. Mark your answer on your answer sheet.

8. Mark your answer on your answer sheet.

○ PART III

Directions: You will hear some conversation between two people. You will be asked to answer three questions about what the speakers say in each conversation. Select the best response to each question and mark the letter (A), (B), (C), or (D) on your answer sheet. The conversation will not be printed in your test book and wiii be spoken only one time.

1. Why did Charles call?

(A) To have a meeting.

(B) To go to the movies.

(C) To do market survey.

(D) To make an invitation.

2. What does the man want the woman to do?

(A) To call him back

(B) To buy a raincoat

(C) To get up early tomorrow

(D) To go to the dinner show with him

3. What does she imply when she says, "Will you give me a rain check?"?

(A) She will meet the other person.

(B) She will never meet him again.

(C) She will cancel her appointment.

(D) She will meet them altogether at the dinner show.

○ PART IV

Directions: You will hear some short talks given by a single speaker, You will be asked to answer three questions about what the

speaker says in each short talk. Select the best response to each question and mark the letter (A), (B), (C) or (D) on your answer sheet. The talks will not be printed in your test book and will be spoken only one time.

1. What is the purpose of this talk?

   (A) To congratulate an employee
   (B) To introduce a new worker
   (C) To handle customer complaints
   (D) To solve the revenue decline

2. Who most likely is the speaker?

   (A) a restaurant manager
   (B) a tech support specialist
   (C) a customer service associate
   (D) a real estate agent

3. What does the speaker imply about chef Dominic?

   (A) He is a chef of many talents.
   (B) He is not good at new recipe.
   (C) He is in charge of cashier.
   (D) He is training a new chef.

4. Which one is not the element to produce a strong Europe?

   (A) technological excellence
   (B) a resonable way of thinking
   (C) a highly educated workforce
   (D) a superior management ability

5. What about the percentage of a world's GDP Europe occupies?

   (A) 12%
   (B) 20%
   (C) 25%
   (D) 30%

6. According to this article, what is the new competition of Asian countries?

   (A) The yen
   (B) The euro
   (C) The dollar
   (D) The pound

Listening Practice 4

● PART I

Directions: For each question in this part, you will hear four statements about a picture in your test book. When you hear the statements, you must select the one statement that best describes what you see in the picture. Then find the number of the question on your answer sheet and mark your answer. The statements will not be printed in your test book and will be spoken only one time.

1.

2.

3.

● PART II

Directions: You will hear a question or statement and three responses spoken in English. They will not be printed in your test book and will be spoken only one time. Select the best response to the question or statement and mark the letter (A), (B), or (C) on your answer sheet.

1. Mark your answer on your answer sheet.

2. Mark your answer on your answer sheet.

3. Mark your answer on your answer sheet.

4. Mark your answer on your answer sheet.

5. Mark your answer on your answer sheet.

6. Mark your answer on your answer sheet.

7. Mark your answer on your answer sheet.

8. Mark your answer on your answer sheet.

○ PART Ⅲ

Directions: You will hear some conversation between two people. You will be asked to answer three questions about what the speakers say in each conversation. Select the best response to each question and mark the letter (A), (B), (C), or (D) on your answer sheet. The conversation will not be printed in your test book and wiii be spoken only one time.

1. What's the occupation of the first man?

(A) He is a doctor.

(B) He is a dentist.

(C) He is an engineer.

(D) He is a pharmacist.

2. What is the problem?

(A) He doesn't know about penicillin.

(B) She has no prescription available now.

(C) Doctors will not give her a prescription.

(D) They are not in good terms with each other.

3. What will she have to do right away?

(A) go to the library

(B) go to the doctor

(C) work in the garden

(D) buy some penicillin

○ PART Ⅳ

Directions: You will hear some short talks given by a single speaker, You will be asked to answer three questions about what the speaker says in each short talk. Select the best response to each question and mark the letter (A), (B), (C) or (D) on

your answer sheet. The talks will not be printed in your test book and will be spoken only one time.

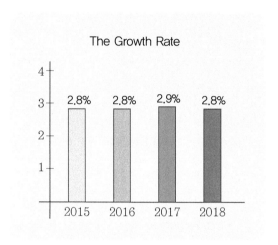

The Growth Rate

1. What about the Korea's GDP world ranking in 2017?

(A) 28th

(B) 29th

(C) 32nd

(D) 42nd

2. Which country is included among the nations superior to Korea in world ranking 2017?

(A) Bahrain

(B) Saudi Arabia

(C) Spain

(D) Germany

3. Look at the graphic. What can be inferred from the chart?

(A) The percentage of growth rate is relatively even.

(B) Lehman Brothers Crisis will never happen again.

(C) GDP is not a global standard any more.

(D) The worldwide economic situation is static.

4. According to this article, how do people spend their time on New Year's Eve?

(A) They want to be alone.

(B) They do not want to go to parties and restaurants.

(C) They eat, drink and dance with their family or friends.

(D) They promise to spend less money or promise to eat less food.

5. Why does people ring bells and blow horns at midnight on New Year's Eve?

(A) Because it is a national holiday.

(B) Because people do not have to work.

(C) To announce that it is time to go home

(D) To celebrate the coming of the New Year

6. Which of the following best describes New Year's Day?

(A) Famous singers sing to the crowd.

(B) People try to be with friends and family.

(C) Many people stay awake until two or three o'clock in the morning.

(D) Everyone thinks about the past year and decides to change their bad habits.

Listening Practice 5

○ PART I

Directions: For each question in this part, you will hear four statements about a picture in your test book. When you hear the statements, you must select the one statement that best describes what you see in the picture. Then find the number of the question on your answer sheet and mark your answer. The statements will not be printed in your test book and will be spoken only one time.

1.

2.

3.

● PART II

Directions: You will hear a question or statement and three responses spoken in English. They will not be printed in your test book and will be spoken only one time. Select the best response to the question or statement and mark the letter (A), (B), or (C) on your answer sheet.

1. Mark your answer on your answer sheet.

2. Mark your answer on your answer sheet.

3. Mark your answer on your answer sheet.

4. Mark your answer on your answer sheet.

5. Mark your answer on your answer sheet.

6. Mark your answer on your answer sheet.

7. Mark your answer on your answer sheet.

8. Mark your answer on your answer sheet.

● PART III

Directions: You will hear some conversation between two people. You will be asked to answer three questions about what the speakers say in each conversation. Select the best response to each question and mark the letter (A), (B), (C), or (D) on your answer sheet. The conversation will not be printed in your test book and wiii be spoken only one time.

1. What are they talking about at the moment?

   (A) Hoover Dam

   (B) Tour program

   (C) Hotel management

   (D) Mechanical engineering

2. When will they arrive at the hotel?

   (A) late at night

   (B) tomorrow morning

   (C) before check-in hours

   (D) around 8 o'clock in the afternoon

3. What do the women want?

   (A) a special event

   (B) a snack for a few minutes

   (C) seven wonders of the world

   (D) a chance to stretch her legs

● PART IV

Directions: You will hear some short talks given by a single speaker, You will be asked to answer three questions about what the speaker says in each short talk. Select the best response to each question and mark the letter (A), (B), (C) or (D) on your answer sheet. The talks will not be printed in your test book and will be spoken only one time.

1. Where can you hear this kind of announcement?

   (A) On the plane.
   (B) At the airport.
   (C) In the terminal building.
   (D) In the hotel dining room.

2. Why should you remain seated until the captain turns off the seat belt sign?

   (A) Because the overhead bins are opened.
   (B) Because the eletronic device can cause an air crash.
   (C) Because the aircraft is not completely parked.
   (D) Because you have onward booking.

3. Which one is NOT true according to the announcement?

   (A) The local time is nine o'clock in the morning.
   (B) Electronic devices can be used until the aircraft is parked at the gate.
   (C) Every passenger should be careful when opening the overhead compartments.
   (D) Every passenger should reconfirm the flight at least 72 hours before departure.

4. What is the applicant going to do?

   (A) Get a new job.
   (B) Graduate from university.
   (C) Get a Master's of Business Administration.
   (D) Work at Yoori International Trading Company.

5. When did the applicant graduate from Halla University?

   (A) About five years ago.
   (B) About four years ago.
   (C) About seven years ago.
   (D) About fifteen years ago.

6. What does he think about his experience in the present company?

   (A) It is hard working but not profitable.
   (B) It has broadened his potential ability.
   (C) It is not good for the Master's degree.
   (D) It is competitive than any other company.

Listening Practice 6

○ PART Ⅰ

Directions: For each question in this part, you will hear four statements about a picture in your test book. When you hear the statements, you must select the one statement that best describes what you see in the picture. Then find the number of the question on your answer sheet and mark your answer. The statements will not be printed in your test book and will be spoken only one time.

1.

2.

3.

○ PART Ⅱ

Directions: You will hear a question or statement and three responses spoken in English. They will not be printed in your test book and will be spoken only one time. Select the best response to the question or statement and mark the letter (A), (B), or (C) on your answer sheet.

1. Mark your answer on your answer sheet.

2. Mark your answer on your answer sheet.

3. Mark your answer on your answer sheet.

4. Mark your answer on your answer sheet.

5. Mark your answer on your answer sheet.

6. Mark your answer on your answer sheet.

7. Mark your answer on your answer sheet.

8. Mark your answer on your answer sheet.

PART Ⅲ

Directions: You will hear some conversation between two people. You will be asked to answer three questions about what the speakers say in each conversation. Select the best response to each question and mark the letter (A), (B), (C), or (D) on your answer sheet. The conversation will not be printed in your test book and wiii be spoken only one time

	Performance hours
Sun. to Wed.	8 p.m.
Thr. to Sat.	11 a.m /8 p.m.
Fri.	-

1. What are they talking about?

   (A) Las Vagas
   (B) Jubilee show
   (C) beautiful singers
   (D) dazzling costumes

2. What is the woman doing now?

   (A) She is helping the man.
   (B) She is setting the schedule.
   (C) She is buying some costumes.
   (D) She is complaining about the program.

3. Look at the graphic. When will the woman watch the show?

   (A) Sunday night
   (B) Wednesday night
   (C) Thursday morning
   (D) Saturday night.

PART Ⅳ

Directions: You will hear some short talks given by a single speaker, You will be asked to answer three questions about what the speaker says in each short talk. Select the best response to each question and mark the letter (A), (B), (C) or (D) on your answer sheet. The talks will not be printed in your test book and will be spoken only one time.

1. What is the writer's private opinion on the custom of tipping?

   (A) The writer thinks that it is fair.
   (B) The writer thinks that it is unfair.
   (C) The writer thinks that it is positive.
   (D) The writer thinks that it is excellent.

2. Where is not expected to leave a tip?

   (A) a hotel room
   (B) a coffee shop
   (C) a barber shop
   (D) a copying shop

3. Which of the following in NOT true according to the above article?

   (A) TIP stands for 'To Insure Promptitude'.
   (B) Today, a person is always expected to leave a tip.
   (C) Samuel Johnson operated a coffee house in London.
   (D) It's a duty of management to pay the maid a sufficient salary.

4. Which one is the best title for the advertisement?

   (A) Moody's and S&P
   (B) Manulife Financial
   (C) Career Opportunity
   (D) Insurance Company

5. Which is not included as a criterion for the
   evaluation of an insurance company?

   (A) service
   (B) profitability
   (C) financial strength
   (D) qualified managers

6. Which of the following is NOT true according to the advertisement?

   (A) Manulife Financial of Canada is
       established in 1987.
   (B) Moody's and S&P are world-famed
       rating agencies.
   (C) The internet site of Manulife is always
       opened to the public.
   (D) Life insurance company is looking
       for excellent branch managers.

Listening Practice 7

○ PART I

Directions: For each question in this part,
you will hear four statements about a
picture in your test book. When you hear
the statements, you must select the one
statement that best describes what you
see in the picture. Then find the number
of the question on your answer sheet
and mark your answer. The statements
will not be printed in your test book and
will be spoken only one time.

1.

2.

3.

○ PART Ⅱ

Directions: You will hear a question or statement and three responses spoken in English. They will not be printed in your test book and will be spoken only one time. Select the best response to the question or statement and mark the letter (A), (B), or (C) on your answer sheet.

1. Mark your answer on your answer sheet.

2. Mark your answer on your answer sheet.

3. Mark your answer on your answer sheet.

4. Mark your answer on your answer sheet.

5. Mark your answer on your answer sheet.

6. Mark your answer on your answer sheet.

7. Mark your answer on your answer sheet.

8. Mark your answer on your answer sheet.

○ PART Ⅲ

Directions: You will hear some conversation between two people. You will be asked to answer three questions about what the speakers say in each conversation. Select the best response to each question and mark the letter (A), (B), (C), or (D) on your answer sheet. The conversation will not be printed in your test book and wiii be spoken only one time.

1. What is Mr. Smith going to do?

   (A) He wants to get a job in the company.
   (B) He wants to quit his job in the company.
   (C) He wants to get an MBA in the university.
   (D) He wants to have an interview with the personnel manager.

2. What is not included in this conversation?

   (A) Job experience
   (B) Family background
   (C) Educational background
   (D) Extra-curriculum activities

3. Who is probably the woman?

   (A) President of USC
   (B) a professor from UCLA
   (C) a student with a law degree
   (D) a director of personnel management

○ PART Ⅳ

Directions: You will hear some short talks given by a single speaker, You will be asked to answer three questions about what the

speaker says in each short talk. Select the best response to each question and mark the letter (A), (B), (C) or (D) on your answer sheet. The talks will not be printed in your test book and will be spoken only one time.

1. What is the topic of this lecture?

(A) Production of linguistic sounds
(B) Theories of second language acquisition
(C) Understanding second language acquisition
(D) Psychological process of the language learner

2. What is not included as an input factor in second language acquisition?

(A) the learner
(B) the learning situation
(C) the uniformity of result
(D) the interaction of the learner and the learning situation

3. Which of the following is NOT true according to this lecture?

(A) Second language acquisition has many interrelated factors.
(B) Second language acquisition is a uniform and predictable phenomenon.
(C) There is no simple way to acquire some knowledge of a second language.
(D) A theory of second language acquisition is to show how many factors are related.

4. What is the correct meaning of 'a white lie'?

(A) A vicious lie to insult other people
(B) An intentional lie to hurt other people
(C) A bad or malicious lie to injure other people
(D) A harmless or innocent lie to avoid hurting people

5. Which of the following is NOT true according to the article?

(A) When a child is young, he is usually taught not to lie.
(B) The world is made up of black & white, not a series of greys.
(C) As a child grows up, he realizes the world is made up of grey.
(D) People can live comfortably together, saying a lot of white lies.

6. Which one does not belong to a white lie?

(A) You look fine.
(B) The new dress is pretty.
(C) I can't go with you because I'm ill.
(D) You should feel guilty about telling lies.

Listening Practice 8

PART I

Directions: For each question in this part, you will hear four statements about a picture in your test book. When you hear the statements, you must select the one statement that best describes what you see in the picture. Then find the number of the question on your answer sheet and mark your answer. The statements will not be printed in your test book and will be spoken only one time.

3.

1.

2.

PART II

Directions: You will hear a question or statement and three responses spoken in English. They will not be printed in your test book and will be spoken only one time. Select the best response to the question or statement and mark the letter (A), (B), or (C) on your answer sheet.

1. Mark your answer on your answer sheet.

2. Mark your answer on your answer sheet.

3. Mark your answer on your answer sheet.

4. Mark your answer on your answer sheet.

5. Mark your answer on your answer sheet.

6. Mark your answer on your answer sheet.

7. Mark your answer on your answer sheet.

8. Mark your answer on your answer sheet.

● PART Ⅲ

Directions: You will hear some conversation between two people. You will be asked to answer three questions about what the speakers say in each conversation. Select the best response to each question and mark the letter (A), (B), (C), or (D) on your answer sheet. The conversation will not be printed in your test book and wiii be spoken only one time.

Flight #	Destination	
KE 012	08:00	
AA 013	10:00	*
AA 014	14:00	*
KE 015	18:00	

(*code share)

1. What is the woman going to do?

   (A) Change flights.
   (B) Sell out flight tickets.
   (C) Book a flight to Hawaii.
   (D) Have a few open seats.

2. Look at the graphic. What did the man recommend?

   (A) the 8:00 flight
   (B) the 10:00 flight
   (C) the 14:00 flight
   (D) the 18:00 flight

3. How will the woman solve the problem?

   (A) She will change the airlines.
   (B) She will take an original one.
   (C) She will change her destination.
   (D) She will take a possible alternative.

● PART Ⅳ

Directions: You will hear some short talks given by a single speaker, You will be asked to answer three questions about what the speaker says in each short talk. Select the best response to each question and mark the letter (A), (B), (C) or (D) on your answer sheet. The talks will not be printed in your test book and will be spoken only one time.

1. What was the final destination of the writer?

   (A) Seoul
   (B) Narita
   (C) Vancouver
   (D) Los Angeles

2. When did the accident begin?

   (A) Three hours after the take off
   (B) Three hours before the landing
   (C) Before the stewardesses served drinks
   (D) When some people were screaming

3. Which of the following is NOT true according to the article?

   (A) The plane was all right at the beginning.
   (B) It was raining hard when the accident happened.
   (C) The passengers were always calm and indifferent.
   (D) Lightning struck one of the engine during the flight.

4. When did she start to study English?

    (A) She studied English during her stay in Hawaii.

    (B) She studied English when she was a fifth grade student.

    (C) She studied English when she was a 16 year-old schoolgirl.

    (D) She studied English when she read books written in English.

5. Which of the following is NOT true according to the article?

    (A) Kim scored 990 points at the 79th TOEIC test in Korea.

    (B) When Kim took the test she was only a middle school student.

    (C) 45 applicants scored 990 points at the 79th TOEIC test in Korea.

    (D) During the stay in Hawaii her English ability was not accelerated.

6. What is the most important thing in learning English?

    (A) To start in an early age

    (B) To stay in Hawaii with family

    (C) To keep in touch with English

    (D) To get a high score in TOEIC test

Listening Practice 9

○ PART I

Directions: For each question in this part, you will hear four statements about a picture in your test book. When you hear the statements, you must select the one statement that best describes what you see in the picture. Then find the number of the question on your answer sheet and mark your answer. The statements will not be printed in your test book and will be spoken only one time.

1.

2.

3.

○ PART Ⅱ

Directions: You will hear a question or statement and three responses spoken in English. They will not be printed in your test book and will be spoken only one time. Select the best response to the question or statement and mark the letter (A), (B), or (C) on your answer sheet.

1. Mark your answer on your answer sheet.

2. Mark your answer on your answer sheet.

3. Mark your answer on your answer sheet.

4. Mark your answer on your answer sheet.

5. Mark your answer on your answer sheet.

6. Mark your answer on your answer sheet.

7. Mark your answer on your answer sheet.

8. Mark your answer on your answer sheet.

○ PART Ⅲ

Directions: You will hear some conversation between two people. You will be asked to answer three questions about what the speakers say in each conversation. Select the best response to each question and mark the letter (A), (B), (C), or (D) on your answer sheet. The conversation will not be printed in your test book and will be spoken only one time.

1. Why was Jenny so late?

(A) She did not want to drive.

(B) Her car broke down again on the road.

(C) She brought about a terrible traffic accident.

(D) Her car blocked up the street on her way home.

2. How long did her father wait?

(A) About two hours

(B) At least one hour

(C) More than three hours

(D) Just for a couple of minutes

3. How does Jenny feel now?

(A) She is satisfied

(B) She is resentful.

(C) She is rather upset.

(D) She is quite assured.

○ PART Ⅳ

Directions: You will hear some short talks given by a single speaker. You will be asked to answer three questions about what the

180

speaker says in each short talk. Select the best response to each question and mark the letter (A), (B), (C) or (D) on your answer sheet. The talks will not be printed in your test book and will be spoken only one time.

1. Which one is the historic site not to see in Rome?

(A) The Vatican

(B) The Parthenon

(C) The Colosseum

(D) The Fountain of Trevi

2. Why does Rome have warm weat–her?

(A) Because it is a peninsular.

(B) Because it has many historic site.

(C) Because it is close to the Atlantic Ocean.

(D) Because it is close to the Mediterra–nean Sea.

3. Which of the following is NOT true accor–ding to the article?

(A) Rome is in southern Italy.

(B) Rome is the capital of Italy.

(C) Rome is close to the Atlantic Ocean.

(D) Rome has about three million people.

4. What is being advertised?

(A) A hotel with a good price

(B) Option for package tourists

(C) A home–stay type of accommodation

(D) An economical way to travel

5. According to the speaker, what is correct about the advertisement?

(A) Customers should stay longer than one night.

(B) Group customers may receive discount.

(C) Customers may ask for a pick–up from airport.

(D) Customers should pay extra for pick–up service.

6. What should the customers do to get a pick–up service?

(A) Make a call beforehand.

(B) Send a note.

(C) Visit online homepage.

(D) No need to do anything.

Listening Practice 10

○ PART I

Directions: For each question in this part, you will hear four statements about a picture in your test book. When you hear the statements, you must select the one statement that best describes what you see in the picture. Then find the number of the question on your answer sheet and mark your answer. The statements will not be printed in your test book and will be spoken only one time.

3.

1.

2.

○ PART II

Directions: You will hear a question or statement and three responses spoken in English. They will not be printed in your test book and will be spoken only one time. Select the best response to the question or statement and mark the letter (A), (B), or (C) on your answer sheet.

1. Mark your answer on your answer sheet.

2. Mark your answer on your answer sheet.

3. Mark your answer on your answer sheet.

4. Mark your answer on your answer sheet.

5. Mark your answer on your answer sheet.

6. Mark your answer on your answer sheet.

7. Mark your answer on your answer sheet.

8. Mark your answer on your answer sheet.

◦ PART Ⅲ

Directions: You will hear some conversation between two people. You will be asked to answer three questions about what the speakers say in each conversation. Select the best response to each question and mark the letter (A), (B), (C), or (D) on your answer sheet. The conversation will not be printed in your test book and wiii be spoken only one time

1. How does the woman want to pay for the computer?

   (A) She wants to pay in cash.
   (B) She wants to pay by credit card.
   (C) She wants to pay in installments.
   (D) She wants to pay by traveler's check.

2. Why does she want to buy Model Number M510?

   (A) Because the man will pay for her.
   (B) Because her computer is our of order.
   (C) Because she can buy it by installments.
   (D) Because she can buy it by discounted rate.

3. How much is the discount rate?

   (A) less than 50%
   (B) more than 50%
   (C) more than 30%
   (D) from 30% to 50%

◦ PART Ⅳ

Directions: You will hear some short talks given by a single speaker, You will be asked to answer three questions about what the

speaker says in each short talk. Select the best response to each question and mark the letter (A), (B), (C) or (D) on your answer sheet. The talks will not be printed in your test book and will be spoken only one time.

1. What is this letter used for?

   (A) To introduce the Radisson Seoul Plaza Hotel.
   (B) To reserve 480 rooms at the hotel.
   (C) To sell out the Radisson Seoul Plaza Hotel.
   (D) To accommodate 1,000 guests at the hotel.

2. What is the maximum capacity of Grand Ballroom and Banquet Halls?

   (A) Up to 480 guests.
   (B) Up to 1,000 guests.
   (C) Up to 1,480 guests.
   (D) Up to 2,480 guests.

3. What is not included in its facilities?

   (A) Royal Suit
   (B) Banquet Hall
   (C) Swimming Pool
   (D) Grand Ball Room

4. What shall we do if we have nothing to declare?

   (A) Go into the red channel.
   (B) Go into the yellow channel.
   (C) Only go through the blue channel.
   (D) Only go through the green channel.

5. Where is this announcement being made?

   (A) In front of customs
   (B) At the police station
   (C) In the supreme court
   (D) At the amusement park

6. Which of the following in NOT true accor-ding to the tourist information?

   (A) You have to declare any goods over the allowances.
   (B) You have to declare any restri-cted or commercial goods.
   (C) At the final destination, you must not declare goods in your hold baggage.
   (D) At the transfer point, you only have to declare goods in your cabin baggage.

Listening Practice 11

○ PART I

Directions: For each question in this part, you will hear four statements about a picture in your test book. When you hear the statements, you must select the one statement that best describes what you see in the picture. Then find the number of the question on your answer sheet and mark your answer. The statements will not be printed in your test book and will be spoken only one time.

1.

2.

3.

Directions: You will hear a question or statement and three responses spoken in English. They will not be printed in your test book and will be spoken only one time. Select the best response to the question or statement and mark the letter (A), (B), or (C) on your answer sheet.

1. Mark your answer on your answer sheet.

2. Mark your answer on your answer sheet.

3. Mark your answer on your answer sheet.

4. Mark your answer on your answer sheet.

5. Mark your answer on your answer sheet.

6. Mark your answer on your answer sheet.

7. Mark your answer on your answer sheet.

8. Mark your answer on your answer sheet.

o **PART III**

Directions: You will hear some conversation between two people. You will be asked to answer three questions about what the speakers say in each conversation. Select the best response to each question and mark the letter (A), (B), (C), or (D) on your answer sheet. The conversation will not be printed in your test book and wiii be spoken only one time.

1. How much does it cost to send the parcel to Los Angeles?

   (A) $12.40
   (B) $12.45
   (C) $20.40
   (D) $20.45

2. Where is this conversation probably taking place?

   (A) at a post office
   (B) at a butcher's shop
   (C) at a computer store
   (D) at a stationery shop

3. Why does she weigh the parcel first?

   (A) To detect the content material.
   (B) Because he refused to sign it.
   (C) Because he didn't fill in the form.
   (D) Because cost usually depends on its weight.

o **PART IV**

Directions: You will hear some short talks given by a single speaker, You will be asked to answer three questions about what the

speaker says in each short talk. Select the best response to each question and mark the letter (A), (B), (C) or (D) on your answer sheet. The talks will not be printed in your test book and will be spoken only one time.

Nationality	The rate of female smokers
Korea	7.3%
UK	26.5%
USA	17.4%
Japan	4.8%

1. What is the main purpose of this talk?

   (A) To notice the danger
   (B) To forecast the weather
   (C) To promote a magic show
   (D) To explain an amusement park

2. What is the distinctive feature of Main Street, U.S.A.?

   (A) Main Street, U.S.A. features many famous cartoon characters.
   (B) Main Street, U.S.A. goes back to a simpler and earlier America.
   (C) Main Street, U.S.A. is the place where the famous movies come to life.
   (D) Main Street, U.S.A. is an area of the more modern advances in the world.

3. Which of the following is NOT true according to the article?

   (A) Certain rides may be unsuitable for pregnant women.
   (B) There is at least one fabulous parade every day of the year.
   (C) Certain rides may not operate due to interruption of electric power.
   (D) You can meet horse-drawn street-cars, moving up and down this street.

4. Which one is the best title for this report?

   (A) Korean high-school boys world's worst smokers!
   (B) Russian high-school girls world's worst smokers!
   (C) The smoking rate of Korean juniors the lowest in the world!
   (D) The smoking rate of Japanese seniors the highest in the world!

5. Which one is NOT true according to this report?

   (A) Korean 18 year-old males had a smoking rate of 41.6%.
   (B) The smoking rate of British high-school girls was the highest.
   (C) The smoking rate of Russian high-school girls was the lowest.
   (D) The Ministry of Education published a booklet, showing the smoking rate.

6. Look at the graphic. Which one is incorrect according to this report?

   (A) Korea
   (B) UK
   (C) USA
   (D) Japan

Listening Practice 12

○ PART I

Directions: For each question in this part, you will hear four statements about a picture in your test book. When you hear the statements, you must select the one statement that best describes what you see in the picture. Then find the number of the question on your answer sheet and mark your answer. The statements will not be printed in your test book and will be spoken only one time.

3.

1.

2.

○ PART II

Directions: You will hear a question or statement and three responses spoken in English. They will not be printed in your test book and will be spoken only one time. Select the best response to the question or statement and mark the letter (A), (B), or (C) on your answer sheet.

1. Mark your answer on your answer sheet.

2. Mark your answer on your answer sheet.

3. Mark your answer on your answer sheet.

4. Mark your answer on your answer sheet.

5. Mark your answer on your answer sheet.

6. Mark your answer on your answer sheet.

7. Mark your answer on your answer sheet.

8. Mark your answer on your answer sheet.

○ PART Ⅲ

Directions: You will hear some conversation between two people. You will be asked to answer three questions about what the speakers say in each conversation. Select the best response to each question and mark the letter (A), (B), (C), or (D) on your answer sheet. The conversation will not be printed in your test book and wiii be spoken only one time.

1. What is the man going to do?

(A) He is going to buy an apartment.

(B) He is going to rent an apartment.

(C) He is going to rent his apartment out.

(D) He is going to move into a new apartment.

2. Who is probably the woman?

(A) a realtor

(B) a curator

(C) a fireman

(D) a chauffeur

3. How much is the reasonable rate per month for the man?

(A) $ 750

(B) $ 850

(C) $ 950

(D) $ 1000

○ PART Ⅳ

Directions: You will hear some short talks given by a single speaker, You will be asked to answer three questions about what the speaker says in each short talk. Select the best response to each question and mark the letter (A), (B), (C) or (D) on your answer sheet. The talks will not be printed in your test book and will be spoken only one time.

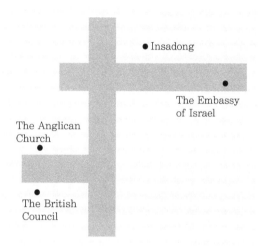

1. Look at the graphic. Where did not Queen Elisabeth Ⅱ visit?

(A) Insadong

(B) The British Council

(C) The Anglican Church

(D) The Embassy of Israel

2. Why was she overwhelmed at her birthday party?

(A) Because of early leaving

(B) Because of the amount of food

(C) Because it was held at the Insa-Dong.

(D) Because the food was shared with people.

3. Which one is NOT true according to the article?

   (A) The Queen stayed in Korea for four days.
   (B) The highlight during her stay was the visit to the Blue House.
   (C) The Queen celebrated her birthday in Hahoe Village, Ahn-Dong.
   (D) The Queen was greatly impressed by the traditional thatched houses.

4. Which one is NOT the covering material of the bottle in this passage?

   (A) Foil
   (B) Cap
   (C) Cork
   (D) Wire

5. Which one is NOT included in the slow opening action of the bottle?

   (A) Remove the aluminum wrapping.
   (B) Turn the cork slowly rather than the bottle.
   (C) Turn the loop in a counter-clock wise direction.
   (D) Hold the bottle firmly with one hand and the cork with the other.

6. Which condition lessens the explosive effects of corkpopping?

   (A) The bottle is kept cold.
   (B) The bottle is kept warm.
   (C) The bottle is agitated so much.
   (D) The bottle is kept upside down.

실전문제 정답

제 1장 단문

1(A)	2(A)	3(A)	4(D)	5(A)	6(A)	7(C)	8(C)	9(C)	10(D)
11(A)	12(A)	13(C)	14(A)	15(B)	16(A)	17(A)	18(B)	19(B)	20(B)
21(A)	22(B)	23(A)	24(A)	25(B)	26(C)	27(A)	28(A)	29(C)	30(C)
31(A)	32(B)	33(B)	34(A)	35(D)	36(C)	37(A)	38(B)		

제 2장 중문

1(B)	2(B)	3(B)	4(A)	5(A)	6(B)	7(C)	8(B)	9(C)	10(D)
11(B)	12(D)	13(B)	14(B)						

제 3장 복문

1(B)	2(B)	3(B)	4(D)	5(C)	6(D)	7(B)	8(B)	9(D)	10(C)
11(A)	12(C)	13(B)	14(C)	15(A)	16(B)	17(D)	18(A)	19(C)	20(B)
21(B)	22(B)	23(B)	24(D)	25(B)	26(B)	27(A)	28(A)	29(B)	30(D)
31(D)	32(C)	33(D)	34(B)	35(D)	36(B)	37(D)	38(B)		

제 4장 명사

1(C)	2(C)	3(D)	4(C)	5(D)	6(A)	7(A)	8(A)	9(D)	10(D)
11(C)	12(B)	13(B)	14(D)	15(D)	16(D)	17(A)	18(D)	19(D)	20(A)
21(B)	22(D)	23(D)	24(A)	25(B)	26(C)	27(D)	28(A)	29(C)	30(D)

제 5장 형용사

1(A)	2(B)	3(A)	4(B)	5(A)	6(B)	7(C)	8(C)	9(B)	10(A)
11(C)	12(B)	13(A)	14(D)	15(B)	16(C)	17(D)	18(A)		

제 6장 동사

1(A)	2(B)	3(A)	4(C)	5(D)	6(D)	7(A)	8(B)	9(D)	10(A)
11(A)	12(B)	13(C)	14(A)	15(A)	16(A)	17(B)	18(A)	19(A)	20(B)
21(A)	22(B)	23(A)	24(D)	25(A)	26(B)	27(A)	28(D)	29(B)	30(C)

제 7장 부사

1(B)	2(C)	3(B)	4(C)	5(A)	6(B)	7(C)	8(C)	9(A)	10(C)
11(A)	12(A)	13(A)	14(A)						

제 8장 대명사

1(A)	2(D)	3(D)	4(A)	5(A)	6(B)	7(A)	8(D)	9(A)	10(B)
11(C)	12(B)	13(A)	14(A)	15(C)	16(B)	17(C)	18(B)	19(A)	20(B)
21(D)	22(C)	23(B)	24(B)

제 9장 전치사

1(A)	2(B)	3(A)	4(A)	5(D)	6(A)	7(B)	8(B)	9(B)	10(C)
11(A)	12(A)	13(C)	14(C)	15(C)	16(C)	17(C)	18(D)	19(A)	20(B)
21(B)	22(B)	23(D)	24(B)	25(A)	26(B)	27(B)	28(D)	29(C)	30(C)

제 10장 준동사

1(B)	2(B)	3(A)	4(B)	5(B)	6(B)	7(A)	8(C)	9(C)	10(A)
11(A)	12(C)	13(A)	14(D)	15(A)	16(A)	17(C)	18(B)	19(B)	20(C)
21(B)	22(C)	23(C)	24(C)	25(A)	26(B)	27(A)	28(A)	29(A)	30(A)

제 11장 비교문

| 1(A) | 2(A) | 3(D) | 4(B) | 5(A) | 6(C) | 7(A) | 8(A) | 9(B) | 10(B) |
| 11(D) | 12(A) | 13(B) | 14(A) | 15(B) | 16(C) | 17(D) | 18(C) |

제 12장 수동문

| 1(A) | 2(D) | 3(A) | 4(C) | 5(B) | 6(A) | 7(A) | 8(C) | 9(B) | 10(A) |
| 11(B) | 12(C) | 13(C) | 14(A) | 15(C) | 16(A) |

제 13장 가정문

1(B)	2(D)	3(B)	4(C)	5(B)	6(C)	7(C)	8(A)	9(C)	10(B)
11(C)	12(A)	13(C)	14(A)	15(B)	16(C)	17(A)	18(B)	19(B)	20(A)
21(C)	22(D)

제 14장 듣기연습

연습 1

Ⅰ. 1(B) 2(C) 3(A)　　Ⅱ. 1(C) 2(B) 3(A) 4(C) 5(A) 6(C) 7(A) 8(B)
Ⅲ. 1(A) 2(B) 3(C)　　Ⅳ. 1(A) 2(A) 3(B) 4(A) 5(D) 6(C)

연습 2

Ⅰ. 1(D) 2(A) 3(C)　　Ⅱ. 1(C) 2(B) 3(A) 4(A) 5(A) 6(B) 7(B) 8(C)
Ⅲ. 1(C) 2(B) 3(A)　　Ⅳ. 1(D) 2(D) 3(D) 4(D) 5(D) 6(C)

연습 3

I. 1(A) 2(C) 3(B)   II. 1(C) 2(A) 3(C) 4(A) 5(C) 6(B) 7(B) 8(B)
III. 1(D) 2(D) 3(A)   IV. 1(D) 2(A) 3(B) 4(B) 5(B) 6(B)

연습 4

I. 1(D) 2(A) 3(C)   II. 1(C) 2(A) 3(A) 4(B) 5(A) 6(B) 7(A) 8(B)
III. 1(D) 2(B) 3(B)   IV. 1(C) 2(D) 3(A) 4(C) 5(D) 6(C)

연습 5

I. 1(B) 2(D) 3(C)   II. 1(A) 2(C) 3(A) 4(B) 5(B) 6(A) 7(C) 8(B)
III. 1(B) 2(D) 3(A)   IV. 1(A) 2(C) 3(B) 4(A) 5(A) 6(B)

연습 6

I. 1(B) 2(A) 3(B)   II. 1(A) 2(A) 3(A) 4(B) 5(C) 6(C) 7(B) 8(B)
III. 1(B) 2(B) 3(D)   IV. 1(B) 2(D) 3(C) 4(C) 5(D) 6(A)

연습 7

I. 1(B) 2(C) 3(D)   II. 1(A) 2(A) 3(C) 4(A) 5(C) 6(B) 7(B) 8(C)
III. 1(A) 2(B) 3(D)   IV. 1(C) 2(C) 3(B) 4(D) 5(B) 6(D)

연습 8

I. 1(C) 2(B) 3(A)   II. 1(A) 2(A) 3(B) 4(C) 5(B) 6(C) 7(A) 8(B)
III. 1(A) 2(D) 3(D)   IV. 1(C) 2(A) 3(C) 4(B) 5(D) 6(C)

연습 9

I. 1(B) 2(C) 3(D)   II. 1(C) 2(C) 3(A) 4(B) 5(A) 6(C) 7(C) 8(A)
III. 1(C) 2(A) 3(C)   IV. 1(B) 2(D) 3(C) 4(C) 5(B) 6(A)

연습 10

I. 1(C) 2(A) 3(D)   II. 1(A) 2(C) 3(B) 4(A) 5(B) 6(B) 7(C) 8(B)
III. 1(C) 2(D) 3(D)   IV. 1(A) 2(B) 3(C) 4(D) 5(A) 6(C)

연습 11

I. 1(C) 2(D) 3(B)   II. 1(C) 2(B) 3(A) 4(B) 5(C) 6(A) 7(C) 8(C)
III. 1(D) 2(A) 3(D)   IV. 1(D) 2(B) 3(C) 4(A) 5(D) 6(D)

연습 12

I. 1(A) 2(B) 3(C)   II. 1(B) 2(B) 3(A) 4(A) 5(B) 6(A) 7(B) 8(A)
III. 1(B) 2(A) 3(A)   IV. 1(D) 2(B) 3(B) 4(B) 5(B) 6(A)

TOEIC Extended

초판1쇄 인쇄 2018년 2월 10일
초판1쇄 발행 2018년 2월 15일

지은이   최우순·송석홍
펴낸이   임 순 재

펴낸곳   (주)한올출판사
등 록   제11−403호
주 소   서울시 마포구 모래내로 83(성산동, 한올빌딩 3층)
전 화   (02)376−4298(대표)
팩 스   (02)302−8073
홈페이지 www.hanol.co.kr
e−메일   hanol@hanol.co.kr

정가 12,000원   ISBN 979−11−5685−629−0